TEXAS

Land of Legend and Lore

TEXAS

Land of Legend and Lore

BILL CANNON

Republic of Texas Press
Dallas • Lanham • Boulder • New York • Toronto • Oxford

Published by Republic of Texas Press
An imprint of The Rowman & Littlefield Publishing Group, Inc.
4501 Forbes Boulevard, Suite 200
Lanham, MD 20706

Distributed by NATIONAL BOOK NETWORK

Library of Congress Cataloging-in-Publication Data

Cannon, Bill.
Texas : land of legend and lore / Bill Cannon.
p. cm.
Includes bibliographical references.
ISBN 1-55622-949-6 (alk. paper)
1. Texas–History–Anecdotes. 2. Texas–History, Local–Anecdotes. 3. Texas–Biography–Anecdotes. 4. Legends–Texas. 5. Folklore–Texas. I. Title.
F386.6.C35 2004
976.4–dc22 2004003415

∞™ The paper used in this publication meets the minimum requirements of American National Standard for Information Sciences–Permanence of Paper for Printed Library Materials, ANSI/NISO Z39.48-1992.

Manufactured in the United States of America.

This book is lovingly dedicated to the memory of A. C. Greene, 1923–2002, who so brilliantly captured the legends and lore of Texas in his "Texas Sketches" column in the *Dallas Morning News* for nearly twenty years, and between the covers of the more than sixty books he authored. I shall remember his vivid revelations of our Texas heritage, and his Christian character, as long as I live.

CONTENTS

★

TWO

TEXAS IS PEOPLE

45

ACKNOWLEDGMENTS

Writing a book with the diversity of a trivia book, especially one featuring the vast state of Texas, requires the assistance and generosity of many individuals and organizations. During the months and years that are required to research, and put into readable focus, each item that is included in this offering, the author has been blessed with the assistance and cooperation of many individuals, organizations, and businesses. We have been helped by more friendly Texans than we could ever acknowledge in the allotted space. This acknowledgment is my small, but sincere, way of saying thanks for your part in bringing this book to fruition. To those whom I am sure to inadvertently omit, I hope that at the time of your contribution I expressed my appreciation adequately! Without the help of the following people and organizations this book would not have been possible: Darren Watkins and his *Mesquite News*, *Eastfield Etcetera* newspaper at Eastfield College, Kent Biffle and the *Dallas Morning News*, Illinois State Guard and Militia Historical Society, Douglas Barnett and the *Handbook of Texas*, the *Champaign-Urbana (IL) News-Gazette*, Norman Krischka, Gene Fowler, *Texas Highways* magazine, the reference staffs at the Irving Public Library, Mesquite Public Library, and Dallas Public Library. Marianne Cannon, Ralph and Ann Poteet of Mesquite, Paul and Virginia Cathey of Mesquite, Joe Baily Motely of Mesquite. Tamara Patterson of Christian Care Center, Mesquite; Elizabeth Heath, Ward County Historical Commission; Richard Roberts, Texas Parks and Wildlife.

INTRODUCTION

Mention the word Texas to a foreigner (a term respectfully used to denote all non-Texans), and it instantly conjures up in their minds the state's most notable legends, like the larger-than-life heroes at the Alamo; the so-called "Black bean death warrants," where captured members of the ill-fated Mier Expedition were forced to draw colored beans from a pot to determine which captive would be executed; the discovery of black gold at Spindletop, which ushered in the age of petroleum and created the misconception of there being a Texas millionaire on every street corner; and, possibly paramount, the "hell-bent-for-leather" episodes of the Texas Rangers.

But it is not only these well-known, and often written-about legends and bits of fascinating lore, that make Texas. There is a myriad of little-known, often forgotten, and sometimes unbelievable events, places, and people that make up the warp and woof of the Texas mystique! This is the Texas of fact and fantasy that so captivates the imaginations of Texans and non-Texans alike! In our previous two books of Texas trivia we have endeavored to expose some of these quirky but true examples of the facts and fantasies that make Texana truly different. In this offering, we gleaned the fields of our trivia collection and once again were rewarded with an abundance of factual examples of oddities and historical rarities that might cause the reader to exclaim, "Only in Texas!"

CHAPTER ONE

FORGOTTEN FOOTNOTES TO TEXAS HISTORY

It's not as if our state's illustrious history needed sprucing up to make it more exciting, or to engender more pride in the Lone Star State, but our investigation into the realm of Texas trivia turned up a number of memorable achievements and historical occurrences that have fallen through the cracks of our memories or have not been brought to our attention. We feel they are worth tacking on to our history as footnotes worth remembering. Most of our state's school-taught history is of nineteenth-century vintage, which accounts for our not being aware of a few of these twentieth-century vignettes. They are, we believe, proof that trivia can also be stimulating.

FIRST MENTION OF OIL IN TEXAS HISTORY

Gerald Ashford's book *Spanish Texas, Yesterday and Today*, published in 1971, tells us that the first mention of Texas oil in history was written by Spanish explorers in 1543, when remnants of

De Soto's expedition sailed seven rickety two-masted ships from Mississippi along the coast to Texas in the direction of Mexico. The author writes, "the voyages came together on a creek on the Texas coast where they smeared the bottoms of their leaky vessels with a 'scum' the sea casts up called copee, which is like pitch, and is used instead of pitch, where that is not to be had." The "scum" was, of course, crude petroleum, which had seeped out under the waters of the Gulf coast and was carried to land by the surf. This is history's first mention of Texas oil.

AMERICA'S FIRST THANKSGIVING (ARGUABLY TEXAS'S MOST CONTROVERSIAL LEGEND)

Although we have written extensively about Texas's claim to being the site of America's first Thanksgiving, in our first Texas trivia book, a book on the legends of Texas would be incomplete without the legend of Texas's claim to Thanksgiving! Perhaps being Texan, we feel we have a God-given right to be more thankful than our other brothers and sisters across the U.S., but just being Texan is not the only reason we can celebrate Thanksgiving with such pride! Would you believe the first Thanksgiving celebrated in America was celebrated right here in Texas? Although tradition and most history books tell us that the first Thanksgiving was celebrated by English colonists in Massachusetts in 1621, some Texans dispute this. El Paso residents say they have written proof that the first Thanksgiving in America was celebrated a full twenty-three years earlier in their city. Based on a poem published in 1610, a decade before the *Mayflower* set sail from England, a thanksgiving feast was held on the banks of the Rio Grande near what is today El Paso. The poem tells the story of Spanish settlers, soldiers, and monks who had exhausted their provisions and water while traveling the Mexican desert en route to what is now New Mexico. Nearly dead from hunger and thirst, they came upon the Rio Grande and with fish and wild game supplied by Indians, they had a feast of Thanksgiving, and a Thanksgiving mass was celebrated. El Pasoans say that this celebration by 500 men, women, and children on April 15, 1598 was the first Thanksgiving held on American soil!

LEGEND OF THE BADGE THAT "KEPT ON A-COMIN' "

Volumes have been written about the exploits of the famed Texas Rangers, who are legends unto themselves. Since their humble beginning in 1823 when impresario Stephen F. Austin hired ten frontiersmen as "rangers" for a punitive expedition against a band of Indians, this one-of-a-kind Texas police agency has been a force to reckon with! Although it was not until November 24th, 1835 that Texas lawmakers instituted a specific force known as the Texas Rangers, the famed law enforcement agency with statewide powers has become as much a part of the Texas mystique as the Alamo, cowboys, and oil wells.

The legends of the individuals who make up this elite band of peace officers are enough to send tremors through the spines and souls of anyone bent on going against Texas law. While the pages of Texas history books fairly explode with the feats of daring performed by Rangers against hostile Indians during the taming of the Texas frontier, the utilization of twentieth-century Rangers to bring law and order to Texas communities where local law

The Texas Ranger badge purported to belong to old-time Ranger Ira Aten. This badge was said to have been carved from a Mexican five peso coin at Aten's instruction in 1883. The name "Ira Aten" is scratched on the back of the badge. The Texas Ranger Hall of Fame and Museum in Waco cannot verify that this was, in fact, Aten's badge, as it has passed through so many hands since Aten retired. They did say it was of the type made for Ira Aten's Ranger company.

enforcers were unable or unwilling to do so fill the newspaper and library archives!

Among those individual legends found in the pages of Texas Ranger lore is the story of how Ranger Captain William J. (Captain Bill) McDonald coined the Texas Ranger motto: "One riot, One Ranger!" This, according to the Texas Ranger Hall of Fame and Museum in Waco, is one of the Ranger legends that is hard to pin down. The motto is generally attributed to Captain William McDonald, but the specific incident prompting the legend is not recorded. Eighty-five-year-old retired Texas Ranger Rufus Van Zandt remembers it as follows in his memoirs: "A riot broke out in Fort Worth (then Camp Worth), and the local authorities telegraphed Austin and asked that a company of Rangers be dispatched. The next day, an engine came barreling into the station, and everybody in town was there to greet the Rangers. A little gray-headed, gray-bearded fellow stepped off the engine and came trotting up the platform. He had two pistols and a sawed-off Winchester about 20 inches long. He said to the mayor, 'I'm Captain Billy McDonald.' The mayor said, 'Where is your company?' " According to Van Zandt, Billy said, "Hell, mayor, you ain't got but one riot."

This is one man's remembrance of the origin of this legendary Texas Ranger motto. There are, no doubt, other versions as to by whom and how the motto originated, but this, too, is part of the Ranger persona that looms so large in the history of Texas! Regardless of its origin, a bronze statue of a Texas Ranger stands in the Dallas municipal airport terminal, Love Field, as a reminder of this bold motto! The statue by Waldine Amanda Tauch is titled "Ranger of 1960: One Riot, One Ranger."

The story you are about to read is about a legend within a legend. Apparently this old-time Ranger, McDonald, had a way with words. He was as quick with words as he was with his six-guns. Bill McDonald's philosophy also became a part of the Texas Ranger legend. Captain McDonald is credited with saying, "No man in the wrong can stand against a fellow that's in the right and keeps on a-comin.' " And 180 years has proved him right! This story is the legend of the highly coveted, and easily recognized,

Texas Ranger badge—the badge that has, for over 120 years, "kept on a-comin' "!

From their inception, Texas Rangers must have recognized that they were an elite cadre of peace officers destined to be a part of Texas history. The men wanted a distinct badge of authority that easily set them apart from all other local law officers, but the star within a circle didn't come into being until the 1870s or 1880s, we are advised by the Texas Ranger Hall of Fame and Museum. By tradition, says its website, Texas Ranger badges are made from Mexican silver five peso coins for sergeants and lieutenants, and the fifty peso gold coins for captains. The five peso coin is known in numismatic circles as "The Cuautemoc," because it bears the image of Indian chief Cuautemoc (ruler of Mexico after Montezuma).

"The custom began," the website goes on to say, "more than 120 years ago when Mexican coins were recognized as a worldwide standard for pure metal and true weight. The oldest authenticated Ranger badge, made in the 1880s, is on display in the Texas Ranger Hall of Fame and Museum in Waco."

The year 2002 was a high point in the history of "the badge that kept on a-comin' "! And I do mean high! Three Ranger badges, one of each rank—captain, lieutenant, and sergeant—were used to symbolize the Rangers' service spanning three centuries, involving horseback, automobiles, and space travel. On June 5, 2002, NASA mission STS-111 to the International Space Station lifted off carrying aboard a piece of Texas history—the world-famous Texas Ranger badges. Lt. Col. Paul Lockhart, pilot of STS-111, and a native of Amarillo, offered to fly the symbol of the Texas Rangers into space to commemorate the forthcoming 180th anniversary of the Texas Rangers.

My friend and former business colleague Ken Aten, of Garland, Texas, is very sentimental about "The badge that kept on a-comin'," and has every right to be. Ken had three great-uncles who were nineteenth-century Texas Rangers and Ken himself once carried a Special Ranger's commission. We are grateful to Ken for permitting us to tell the story of what is purported to be his uncle, Ira Aten's, Texas Ranger badge. The Atens, who made the Rangers a family affair, were Ira, Calvin, and Eddie. In an interview with Ken, we were told how Ira Aten's grandson, Gary Radder of Alamo, California recently tracked down what is purported to be his grandfather's original Ranger badge. No small miracle, considering that Ranger Ira Aten served from April 13 until August 20, 1889. The badge was carved from a silver five peso coin at Ira's instruction in 1883. The historic Ranger artifact has passed through many hands over the last 120 years, and officials at the Texas Ranger Hall of Fame and Museum tell us that the badge has the appearance of badges made for Ira Aten's Ranger company, but they cannot verify it belonged to Ranger Aten. After Ira Aten's death in 1953, the badge was taken by one of his sons, Ira D. Aten, who gave it to a friend in San Diego who was a collector. The badge was next seen in the spring of 1978 at a Western-Americana show in San Jose, California, where it was given or traded for some cartridges. Imogene Aten, Ira's only child, was able to identify the badge because Ira had scratched his name on the back of the silver badge. The historic old badge changed hands several times before it finally ended up in family hands. Ira Aten's grandson, Gary Radder, indicated in a letter that the badge was sent to the Texas Ranger Hall of Fame and Museum to be authenticated. The photo of Ranger Ira Aten's badge reflects the stark simplicity that characterizes the first hand-crafted Ranger badges. But those who lived outside the law knew not to mistake this simplicity for weakness, for this was the badge worn by the men who kept on a-comin'!

DAVY CROCKETT'S AUDACIOUS FAREWELL

One of the best-known heroes of the Alamo was a Tennessean who fought in the Creek War with Andrew Jackson in 1813. He served three terms in the U.S. Congress and when defeated for a fourth in 1835, he reflected his feelings about the lack of appreciation shown by his constituents in his audacious parting remarks. In typical backwoodsman fashion, Davy Crockett's farewell was this: "You all can go to hell, and I will go to Texas," which he did just in time to join in the defense of the Alamo.

SUNRISE ON THE MOUND: THE LEGEND AND LORE THAT SURROUNDS FLOWER MOUND'S NAMESAKE

Eric Sipos, writing of the town of Flower Mound in the *Lewisville News*, states, "Like the town itself, the Easter Sunrise Service, on the town's namesake attracts more people each passing year." Mr. Sipos goes on to say that "This year the service is expected to draw more than 500 people."

Flower Mound was settled in the 1830s, and the mound itself was used as a campsite, according to Alton Bowman, director of the Mound Foundation. "The mound was always called Flower Mound, and as the early settlers came here they used the mound for camp meetings, which would last two or three weeks. During that time preachers would come in for worship services," Bowman said. According to legend, settlers wanted to build the first church on the mound, but were warned not to by local Indians. It seems that the mound held religious significance to Wichita Indians as well as to early settlers. Mr. Bowman noted: "It is said that some Wichitas are buried in the mound."

Regardless of the legend that surrounds this rise of ground in Flower Mound, one certainty is that it has turned into a beautiful and fitting place to celebrate the meaning of the promise of new life. Each spring from its lofty, flower-covered height come echoes of inspiring songs of Christian praise, and the Word of God on Easter morning. A debt of gratitude is owed to the town of Flower Mound, and especially to the Flower Mound Summit Club, for perpetuating this inspiring presentation of this important symbol of Christianity to its residents and many guests alike! I am also grateful that my thoughtful son-in-law, Bill Binnig, selected this historical and progressive Denton County town with the wildflower-bedecked mound in which to raise my precious grandchildren. My hope is that they will enjoy many inspiring Easter sunrise services atop the town's historic namesake!

RUNAWAY SCRAPE

Following the defeat of the Texas troops at the Alamo, Sam Houston pulled his Texian troops toward the Texas coast as the Mexican army advanced. Civilians fled before the advancing Mexican army. This tactical retreat ordered by Sam Houston, and the flight of the settlers southward, is known as the Runaway Scrape.

Houston's conduct of the revolutionary war was criticized by his detractors, but his subsequent quick and decisive victory at San Jacinto more than justified his actions as a battlefield commander. Historical revisionists have subsequently insisted that Houston had arranged for U.S. troops to intercept the retreating Mexicans, and that Houston was intentionally leading the Mexican army into the jaws of a trap. San Jacinto proved that the Texas general needed no outside help to bring victory to the Texians. With the battle cry "Remember the Alamo, Remember Goliad" on their lips and in their hearts, the Texians swarmed over the Mexicans, bringing them sudden death, and bringing Texas its independence from a tyrannical Mexico!

DID YOU EVER WONDER WHAT HAPPENED TO THE DEFEATED MEXICAN GENERAL SANTA ANNA?

We have often been asked what happened to Santa Anna after the Texians soundly trounced the Mexican army at San Jacinto. For accurate information about this brutal Mexican dictator and general I turn to the *Handbook of Texas*. Most Texas history buffs know how the Mexican general was captured following the Battle of San Jacinto, disguised in peasant clothes, and was unwittingly exposed by his own men when brought to Sam Houston. Recognizing their commanding officer, the soldados began to demonstrate their praise of him, shouting "Excelencia! Excelencia!" Following capture by Sam Houston's army, the Mexican general was sent to Washington, D.C., and was then returned to Mexico.

Santa Anna retired to his estate at Magna de Clevo for a time and emerged to join in the defense of Mexico against the French in 1838, in what was known as "The Pastry War." He lost a leg in battle, and buried his dismembered leg. After the "Pastry War" Santa Anna regained his popularity and was acting president of Mexico in 1839, having overthrown Bustamante. From 1841 to

1845 Santa Anna was dictator of Mexico. Excesses led to his being overthrown and exiled to Havana, Cuba. When the former dictator fell out of favor, he attempted to have his leg disinterred and placed in a Mexican museum in an attempt to re-establish his popularity by establishing a cult following.

At the beginning of the Mexican-American War, Santa Anna entered into negotiations with U.S. president James K. Polk, offering a possibility of settlement, and was permitted to enter Mexico through the American blockade. When negotiations failed and the United States captured Mexico City, Santa Anna retired to exile, living in Cuba, the Dominican Republic, and Nassau. During that time he finally abandoned politics and wrote his memoirs. In 1874 he was permitted to return to Mexico City, where he lived in obscurity until his death in 1876. (See "Spoils of War Can Be Strange: Santa Anna's Leg Captured in Mexican-American War" in chapter 4 of this book.)

THE LONG AND SHORT OF IT IN EARLY TEXAS

Believe it or not, whether early Texians were buying land or fabric to make a dress, the measurements were influenced by Mexican rule over Tejas y Coahuila. We have compiled a few facts about Mexican measurements that affected Texas settlers.

The very first Mexican measurements that confronted Norteamericanos wishing to settle in Texas were "a league and a labor." These Spanish land measurements were used in making Mexican land grants to immigrants. The Colonization Act under which Stephen F. Austin's "Old Three Hundred" settled in Texas allowed land grants as follows: the heads of families engaged in farming received a labor (177 acres) of land, and cattle raisers received a sitio, or league, of land (4,428 acres). Most settlers combined farming with ranching and received a league and a labor of land.

Many old Texas land deeds reflect a survey measuring in vrs.: "15 vrs. North and 20 vrs. West." "Vrs." stood for the Spanish measurement varas. One vara is approximately thirty-three and one-third inches. 5,654.4 square varas equal one acre. 1,906.1 vrs.

equal one mile. Originally a vara meant a long, thin branch of a tree or plant. Later it came to mean any straight stick or lance. It eventually became used as a measuring stick, and later a measurement. Perhaps not so important as land measurement, but certainly important to the women sewing for the family, was the measurement of a yard. While Texas was under Spanish rule the yard was thirty-three inches. It was not until 1832 that merchantmen introduced the English measurement of thirty-six inches to a yard.

THE LEGEND OF THE BLOOD-RED FIELDS OF MONTAGUE'S GROVE

After seventy-odd years of traversing the highways and back roads of the Lone Star State and witnessing nature's splendor, especially her palette of wildflowers that perennially blanket the fields and hills of Texas each year, I am confident the rich red color of what is known as Montague's Grove near the Grayson County city of Sherman is nature's perennial display of Indian paint brushes and Indian blankets rather than a phenomenon resulting from a skirmish with a band of Indians that happened in the mid-nineteenth century.

This botanical explanation of the "blood-red" fields of Montague's Grove is not nearly so exciting as the little-known legend so vividly recounted by Mattie D. Lucas and Mita H. Hall in their book *A History of Grayson County*, published in 1936. According to these two chroniclers of Grayson County history, the last battle with the Indians in what is now Grayson County is said to have occurred in 1843 in a large grove just south of the present city of Sherman on the old Howe Road. A band of Indians had been moving around the country, robbing the settlers and making away with horses. On one occasion they camped for the night in this grove—a decision that was to prove deadly! Daniel Montague, Fannan County surveyor, with a band of men, followed them and attacked them in the early morning, killing almost the entire band—about sixteen. There was a legend afterwards that so much blood was spilled on the grass, the flowers next year were bright red in color. The grove was called Montague's Grove.

ORIGIN OF THE WORD "CHAPS"

Chaparral is the name given to a dense thicket of shrubs known as evergreen oaks. These thickets are widely spread on the plains of the Southwest. In order to prevent being stuck or scratched while riding through the chaparral, Mexican vaqueros (cowboys) buckled on a leather pantlike covering called "chaparreras." It is from this Spanish word that the modern English word "chaps" is derived.

DALLAS'S FIRST INTERSTATE HIGHWAY

The discovery of Dallas's first Interstate Highway truly qualifies as "A Forgotten Footnote to Texas History"! On a recent foray into the West End, Dallas's upbeat entertainment section in the former warehouse section of downtown Dallas, we discovered a historical marker buried among the restaurants, clubs, and eclectic shops, and lighted only by the garish neon signs advertising nearby bars designed to attract excitement-craving young people. The marker is lost to all West End devotees, the most of whom are attracted only to the here and now, and on whom Texas's and Dallas's history is lost!

The marker is located in the 1800 block of North Market Street. It relates to us the history of the Central National Road of the Republic of Texas, as follows: "During the early days of the Republic of Texas, settlers and pioneers coming to Texas from the United States, entered Texas by crossing the Red River in northwest Red River County. On the north side of the crossing was the terminus of a U.S. military highway in 1844. The Congress of the Republic of Texas appointed a commission to lay out a road connecting the crossing on the Red River to the Trinity River in central Dallas County."

The *Handbook of Texas* explains the project this way: "The road was to begin on the bank of the Trinity River, not more than fifteen miles below the bank of the Elm Fork, in Dallas County, and run to the northwest corner of Red River County, to the south bank of the Red River, opposite the mouth of the Kiamachi River. As surveyed, the Central National Road probably started at the John Neely Bryan crossing on the Trinity River, a little north of the later site of the Dallas County courthouse, ran east by north to the Dallas County line."

This reference book leads us to believe that the Central National Road was Dallas's first Interstate Highway. Actually, considering the geography at the time, it was an international highway, connecting the Republic of Texas with the United States. The *Handbook* goes on to say, "To the north and east the Central National Road connected to the military road to Fort Gibson and old roads connecting Jonesborough with settlements in Arkansas. At its southern terminus it connected with the road opened in 1840 between Austin and Preston Bend on the Red River, in effect making it an international highway between St. Louis and San Antonio."

It is difficult for we modern-day Dallasites to imagine that with the millions of tons of concrete and asphalt that form the modern interstates, freeways, toll roads, and elevated highways that have become the arteries that route the flow of the city's traffic, we had our very first interstate over 150 years ago.

GOT CHANGE FOR A "COW AND A CALF"?

It is difficult in today's money-driven economy to think of money as being trivial. However, in scanning our history of Texas and the lore attached to it, we find numerous money-related pieces of lore that have, over the years, become victims of our dimming memories. We want to use this book as a forum to reacquaint our readers with some interesting money-related Texas truths.

There was a time in Texas when having a cow and a calf was like having a "sawbuck" in the pocket of your jeans. The *Handbook of Texas* reminds us that during the days of the Republic of Texas, notes signed by individuals promising to pay a cow and a calf passed as ten-dollar bills, even though a cow and a calf weren't worth ten U.S. dollars

Two-bits, four-bits, six-bits: we all grew up using these slang expressions when referring to American coinage. But few of us realized that these terms were of Texas origin. It was very important for early Texans to know what "one bit" was, because some river ferries listed the rate for transporting one small animal, say a hog, as "one bit." This brings about the origin of the slang terms we use today. Coins were a rarity in America, especially in Texas during its colonization. Early Texas colonists used the Spanish silver dollar, known as "pieces of eight." These coins could actually be cut into eight pie-shaped pieces. These pieces were called "bits." Each bit was worth 12½ cents in American money. When the U.S. coined the quarter, it was worth, naturally, two bits. The U.S. half dollar was worth four bits, and so on. The familiar word peso, used to identify Mexican money, is actually an abbreviation for the phrase "peso de ocho," meaning a piece, or the weight, of an eight! There are times today when we think our money is only worth a fraction of what it once was. This trivia item proves that fractional money was necessary in early Texas.

A post office department was established by decree of the Republic of Texas provisional government and approved by an act of the Texas Congress dated December 20, 1836. The first postal rates established in Texas were 6¼ cents for up to 20 miles, 12½ cents up to 50 miles, and 18¾ cents up to 100 miles. The rate for 200 miles was 25 cents, and 37½ cents for further distances. As Spanish money was used, the fractions created no difficulty. These rates were for one-page letters. The letter was folded over with the address on the front; envelopes did not come along until 1845. Strong penalties were initiated to deter robberies from the mail. The first offense of robbery of the mail called for a prison term of not more than ten years, and anyone foolish enough to be involved in a second offense was sentenced to death by hanging. We hope you are as fascinated by these bits of Texas money trivia as we are. We find the legends and lore of Texas money priceless!

THE TEXAS POLL TAX

What's a "poll tax"? If you voted in Texas from 1903 until the elections of 1964, you paid a fee known as a poll tax before you could vote! Ranging from as little as fifty cents to as much as two dollars, this tax to exercise your right to vote disenfranchised a large segment of the Texas population, until the tax was repealed by the U.S. Congress and this was ratified by the Texas Legislature. Texas Negroes could ill afford not to have representation on a state and federal level of government but were financially unable to ante up the poll tax fee, small as it was. Some who could afford the tax revolted and gave up their vote rather than pay a fee for a right they felt was guaranteed to them as American citizens. Although it was a common opinion that the poll tax was initiated to prevent Negroes and poor whites from controlling local elections, many disputed this opinion. The *Texas Almanac* for 2002–2003 bears out the effect the poll tax had on American Negroes with this quotation: "Historians differ on whether the levy was designed to keep blacks or poor whites—or both—from voting. Certainly the poll tax cut election turnouts. Black voter participation dropped from about 100,000 in the 1890s to an estimated 5000 in 1906."

In gathering material for this item, I was surprised at the number of people who did not know what the poll tax was. We had to be sure we were talking to folks who were adults prior to 1960. One anecdotal bit of Texas trivia flashed across my mind as I gathered this almost forgotten footnote to Texas history. When popular radio personality and flour salesman W. Lee "Pappy" O'Daniel ran for governor of Texas, he wasn't able to vote for himself because he had failed to pay his poll tax for that year. Whether O'Daniel had refused to pay the tax or had just neglected this important duty is not recorded. But what is on record is that the candidate promised to repeal the poll tax if elected.

WHY QUARTER HORSES ARE SO NAMED

So much of the Texas mystique centers around the cowboy and his lifestyle, which, in great measure, includes his horse. It would, we think, be an oversight to write about Texas without including some facts about horses. A favorite among Texas cowboys, whether working cattle or simply demonstrating their horsemanship in a rodeo, is the American Quarter Horse. According to the American Quarter Horse Heritage Center in Amarillo, this breed of horse was a cross between the American colonists' English thoroughbreds and the Spanish horses brought to America by the Spanish explorers. The horse was bred for fast speed over short distances. Having no racetracks, the colonists raced their horses on public roads and streets. Their most popular race was a quarter of a mile. The American colonists found the new breed especially adept at the quarter-mile sprint; thus they named the breed "the quarter horse." The horse also has innate cow sense, thus making them valuable to ranching and cattle operations. The naming of this Texas icon dates back to colonial times in America.

One of America's most famous quarter horses was Sam Houston's "Copper Bottom." Houston had him sent to him from Pennsylvania. It is said that Copper Bottom's offspring were much sought after. A more infamous quarter horse was known as "The Denton Mare." This was a racehorse owned by the Texas outlaw Sam Bass. In addition to being a bank and stage robber, the outlaw was a horse trainer and raced the Denton Mare named Jenny. Jenny was said to be a descendant of the famous quarter horse Steel Dust.

HORSE FACTS: As most Texans know, horses are measured in hands. It is said, for example, a horse is fifteen hands high. A "hand" is the width of an average human hand—four inches is the accepted measurement. A horse is measured from the ground to the horse's withers. The withers is the highest part between the horse's shoulder blades. The front part of a saddle usually sits at the withers. If a horse measures fifteen hands high he is sixty inches from the ground to the withers, or five feet high.

GIMME THAT OL' TIME RELIGION!

Occasionally a special Texas story comes across our desk that is so revealing about those early days in the Lone Star State that we can hardly wait to share it with our friends, especially our readership. Such is the case with a lovingly written story by Larita Pierson, whose byline can often be found in the *Antique Almanac*, published in Whitewright, Texas. We are grateful to the *Almanac* and Larita Pierson for giving us permission to publish her well-researched insights into the pioneer days of her forefathers in her beloved North Texas.

This is the story of pioneer worship services in the mid-1800s and early 1900s. Ms. Pierson reminds us that Mexican land grants in Texas required swearing allegiance to Mexico and professing the Catholic faith. Usually this was simply lip service, however; most of the immigrants coming to the Texas Blacklands from the southern Bible Belt of Tennessee and Kentucky were Protestant, Bible-oriented orthodox Christians—usually Baptist, Methodist, Presbyterian.

As was the case in first-century Christianity, the first church services were held in homes and were nondenominational. Like the first schools, the first Texas churches were log cabins furnished with benches made from split logs. These first chapels were usually built by a landowner on his own property and served his own family and his neighbors. The congregations were divided with men and boys sitting on one side of the church, and women, girls, and babies on the other. Since the gathering place was regarded as sacred, no conversation was allowed before services began. Hymn books were scarce; usually only the preacher and song leader had copies. More often the songs that were sung were those the congregation knew by heart. They were revival songs like "Are You Washed in the Blood," "At the Cross," "There Is a Fountain," "Shall We Gather at the River"; songs of petition, like "My Faith Looks Up to Thee," "Sweet Hour of Prayer," "Nearer My God to Thee"; and songs of joyous assurance, like "What a Friend We Have in Jesus," "Bringing In the Sheaves," and "We Are Bound for the Promised Land." The entire congregation knelt during prayer.

Union churches followed the log cabin chapels. Several denominations, usually the four predominant ones, Methodist, Baptist, Presbyterian, and the Church of Christ would build a church building. Each group would provide a preacher for each Sunday of the month. The Methodist circuit riding preachers would often have several of these churches, preaching at a different location on each consecutive Sunday.

A young boy at the time who attended Sunday School and preaching described one such church. "There were three churches, Baptist, Methodist, and Presbyterian. The Presbyterians read the sermon and it was long. Under one and a half hours being thought brief. The longer they were, the more pleasing the comments from the grownups. But us children who had attended a sunday School from 9 to 10 o'clock, had to sit and listen until 12:30 or one o'clock on 'the whole duty of man.' The Baptists and Methodists were briefer and more extemporaneous."

Not all communities were blessed with union churches, however. A young Greenville lawyer whose father was a Baptist minister wrote to his brother back home in Virginia: "We have no regular preaching. The Methodists and Campbellites (a name given to the Church of Christ members because they were under the leadership of Alexander Campbell), and once in awhile the Baptists preach here, but not every Sunday. The Campbellites stick together. They are intensely dogmatic, egotistical, and intolerant. The Methodist circuit rider preaches here regularly every fourth Sunday. They are the same sort of Methodists found everywhere, and by the way, they all seem to be alike in appearance wherever they are found. The Baptists preach here only by chance." On another occasion he wrote, "The sound of preaching is rattling on my ears on every side. The Campbellites are carrying on a meeting in the Court House, and the Negroes in a house a short distance from my office. We Baptist's have no regular preaching. Only when a missionary comes do we go to church."

By the 1870s, the population of the "Four Corners" (the extreme north of Texas) had grown enough that the individual denominations were able to begin building their own churches, and each began to draw sharper lines regarding doctrine. Yet the physical limitations of those early buildings led to practices that forestalled total separation by denomination. With no facility for submersion for baptism, sometimes the whole community would gather at the river, farm pond, or even gin pool pond for baptismal services. It was a great social and religious activity for small town folks, representing the saving of a soul and a chance to meet friends and associates. The lack of effective cooling brought congregations outdoors, where summer services were held under brush arbors. When the cotton was laid by at the end of August, camp meetings and revivals were held. People gathered from miles around and spent the time in worship, song, and spiritual renewal, while catching up on all the news from friends and family countywide.

TEXAS WELCOMES EARLY MAIL AND PASSENGER STAGE

In their fine book *A History of Grayson County,* authors Mattie D. Lucas and Mita H. Hall provide a graphic look at what was to be one of Texas's earliest and best-known stage lines, the Butterfield Overland Stage. Their word picture of the role played by this stage line in the lives of early Texas settlers prompted us to review the stage line's history in the *Handbook of Texas*. The following is the Overland Stage Line's story taken from both works: "The crowning event of this period of our country's history (1846–1861)," write Lucas and Hall, "was the coming of the Overland mail. The United States government entered into a contract with John Butterfield and associates to operate the first mail route connecting the eastern United States with the west. The line began at Saint Louis and at Memphis uniting at Fort Smith, and continued to San Francisco. A six-year contract was given at $600,000 a year for semi-weekly mail. The service was to begin September 15, 1858. The contract was dated Sept. 16, 1857." The company was allowed to choose its own route. The route chosen by Butterfield was the longest route using horse-drawn conveyances in U.S. history—2,795 miles—756 of which were in Texas. Its route across northern Texas, according to the *Handbook of Texas*, began at Colbert's ferry on the Red River, and continuing westward to Franklin (now El Paso). *A History of Grayson County* tells us, "Stations were to be provided every ten or twenty miles, where mail could be picked up and deposited; the trip was to be made in less than 25 days. Each station was to include a keeper's house, a stable, a blacksmith shop, and eating houses."

That same book offers an interesting commentary on the Indians of Texas and the Butterfield Overland Mail stages: "Horses were used for the coaches until they reached Fort Belknap—then mules—the chief reason being, that the Indians would attack the stage in order to get the horses, but they wouldn't have the mules as a gift!"

DEATH OF THE "IRON QUEEN": A LEGEND OF BOOM AND BUST IN EAST TEXAS!

Few Texans are unfamiliar with "Boom or Bust" times in Texas. The fame of the Lone Star State's petroleum industry has spanned the globe and the words Texas and "black gold" are synonymous. The bringing in of a new oil field in Texas usually resulted in boomtowns and boomtimes—terms that reflected growth and prosperity beyond all expectations. The state is dotted with cities and towns that have enjoyed, if only for a season, the explosive growth and prosperity that equaled the eruptive force of a gusher signaling the discovery of yet another oil field.

Kilgore, Ranger, Midland, Odessa, and Beaumont were all cities born from the gushing womb of Texas oil derricks. All suckled at the bosom of fossil fuel deposits under the crust of Texas's earth. The mortality rate of Texas "boomtowns" was, as in the case of humans, dependent on many factors. Many are still flourishing and in maturity are equally prosperous, while some have dried up like the long-since-capped wells that gave them birth.

The petroleum story of Texas is a well-documented history and requires no half-soling from this writer. But the boom and bust of one East Texas town, which was once called "The Iron Queen of the Southwest," is a legend that does need exposing to fresh air. Few are as familiar with the iron boom in East Texas as with the tales of the Texas oil fields that ushered America into the petroleum age. My chance meeting with Blondy Hugghins, who was born near the Cherokee County town of Rusk, opened my eyes to another Texas boom and bust in the short-lived industrial town of New Birmingham. Its name alone conjures up images of blast furnaces, molten slag, pigs of iron, and the constant pounding of giant hammers forming white hot metal into a myriad of forms. John's vivid description of the beautiful Southern Hotel, called by some "The most modern hotel West of the Mississippi," was enough to send me scurrying to my well-used *Handbook of Texas* to explore this long-extinct East Texas industrial town in more detail.

I was informed by the *Handbook of Texas* that "New Birmingham was founded in the 1880s by sewing machine salesman, Alexander Blevins, who was impressed by the large iron deposit in the area and the already operating foundry at the Rusk Penitentiary." Salesman Blevins was not the first to be impressed with the county's iron ore deposits. The *Handbook of Texas*'s information about the Rusk Penitentiary includes the fact that the penitentiary was built "between 1877 and 1883 to relieve overcrowding at the State penitentiary in Huntsville, and to employ convicts in the development of iron ore resources in East Texas."

The Alabama-bred salesman optimistically envisioned the town as an industrial town comparable to Birmingham in his home state. With the backing of several capitalists, Blevins was able to form the Cherokee Land and Iron Company. By 1888, Blevins was able to take an option on 20,000 acres of land rich in iron ore deposits. Mining started immediately and a blast furnace and rolling mill were soon constructed. The streets of New Birmingham were platted near the Kansas and Gulf Short Line Railroad. The town grew, with businesses and soon residences sprouting up in the new town. "The centerpiece of the businesses," says the *Handbook of Texas*, "was the five-story, brick Southern Hotel, which featured running hot and cold water, electric lights, and an elegant restaurant." Among the hotel's guests during its heyday were President Grover Cleveland, Governor James Stephen Hogg, and railroad magnate Jay Gould. The new Texas town was highly publicized, with one newspaper heralding the town as "The future manufacturing center of the Southwest."

The inability to find new capital and, coincidentally, an omen of sorts resulted in the gradual decline of New Birmingham. The "omen" was the result of an occurrence in July of 1890, when William Hammons, one of the venture's chief backers, was gunned down by a local businessman, who thought Hammons had insulted his wife. Hammons's wife, after learning of her husband's death, was reported as "running through the streets, calling on God to leave no stone or stick standing" in the town. In later years, many saw her plea as an omen. Mrs. Hammons's wish for New Birmingham came true! Without additional financial backing, the promoters of the town were unable to weather the panic of 1893. To add to the troubles, in that same year an explosion and fire destroyed Blevins's blast furnace, throwing almost 300 residents out of work. The Southern Hotel and most of the manufacturing plants closed, and in a short time merchants and residents began moving away. On July 4th, 1893, the *Cherokee County Banner* announced that the "Iron Queen" was dead. By 1910, New Birmingham had been abandoned.

CRACKING THE WHIP ON "JOHN BARLEY CORN" IN TEXAS

Not willing to tackle the forces of "Do-Gooders" who have made it their calling to rid Texas society of the evils fostered by strong drink, we are shying away from publicly castigating those organized forces and self-anointed individuals whose mission in life was to save the menfolk of Texas from the destruction of self and family by the abolition of whiskey, which they deemed to be the root cause of most marital disorders.We will, however, include in our history topics this review of the history of some of the better-known efforts directed toward abolition of strong drink in Texas.

The most widely known and best-organized effort in the direction of prohibition in Texas was the Woman's Christian Temperance Union (WCTU), which made its Texas debut in a tour of the state between 1881 and 1883. The organization made great inroads in the prohibition movement in Texas, establishing both white and black unions.

But, strong as the WCTU was, the best-remembered prohibitionist in Texas (probably because of the sensationalism attached to her efforts) was Carry Amelia Nation (1846–1911). The very name Carry Nation conjured up visions of total destruction in the minds of barkeeps throughout Texas. Mrs. Nation, who was born in Kentucky, and raised in Kentucky and Missouri, was the victim of a marriage ruined by her husband's alcoholism. Carry Nation had numerous mystic experiences. After undergoing a religious conversion at a revival meeting, she believed she had been elected by God and spoke with divine inspiration. She became a human dreadnought in her fight against the evils of hard liquor! Carry Nation's fight against whiskey is best remembered by her adoption in 1900 of the hatchet, which she employed to wreck "joints" that sold whiskey and tobacco. Her sale of miniature hatchets for souvenirs and money earned on her speaking tours enabled her to pay the fines she was assessed as a result of her more than thirty arrests.

But Carry Nation was not the only female prohibitionist to resort to violence in an attempt to derail the sale of booze in Texas! One *Dallas Morning News* story, dated March 21, 1896, and bearing a dateline of Ladonia, Texas, captured our attention with the following blaring headline: "Respected Ladies Crack Their Whips." The article about the Fannin County town of Ladonia reads as follows: "This afternoon, March 20, 1896, a party of twenty highly respected ladies came into the railroad station room of the Santa Fe and severely cowhided Dr. Hancock, a physician who recently came here from Bonham. The party of ladies demanded of him that he leave town and promise not to return. He told them he would not do it. They showed him a dozen cowhides (whips) and informed him they would be used on him if he did not leave town and quit writing prescriptions for whiskey. (Ladonia was as dry as a horny toad's belly.) He again refused. When a dozen cowhides were drawn and 500 lashes were administered to the doctor he left at once for Honey Grove fifteen miles to the north. Quite a crowd gathered at the depot while the thrashing was in progress. Excitement was intense. They were the same ladies who entered a malt tonic joint here last Saturday and prayed for the proprietor and pleaded with him to close."

This item ran the next day, datelined Bonham, the Fannin County courthouse town: "Dr. Hancock, cowhided at Ladonia, arrived here last night and shows that he was badly used up. County Attorney JC Meade says that the case will be fully investigated and all the guilty parties punished. The following parties appeared before the county judge by proxy, and pleaded guilty to aggravated assault and were each fined $25." Names of twenty-one highly respected ladies were listed.

BIG TEXAS AND "LITTLE TEXAS" HELP CARRY ROOSEVELT TO THE WHITE HOUSE

One of the best-known names in U.S. military history is "The Rough Riders" of Spanish-American War fame (1898). Officially the First United States Volunteer Cavalry, "The Rough Riders," under the command of Colonel Theodore (Teddy) Roosevelt, also carried the sobriquets "Teddy's Terrors" and "The Rocky Mountain Rustlers." This legendary fighting unit was, according to the *Handbook of Texas*, "an aggregation of cowboys, Indian fighters, outlaws, Eastern Aristocrats, and Ivy League athletes."

Roosevelt lauded the abilities of the famed Texas Rangers who helped make up the unit. "We drew a great many recruits from Texas," said Roosevelt. "From nowhere did we get a higher average, for many of them had served in that famous body of frontier fighters, the Texas Rangers. These rangers needed no teaching, they were trained to obey and take responsibility."

Roosevelt joined his regiment on May 16 in San Antonio, where the men, encamped in what is now Roosevelt Park, trained for their role in the invasion of Cuba. They also bought horses in San Antonio.

In Dale Walker's book *The Boys of '98*, we learned what part "Little Texas" played in Teddy Roosevelt's life. In writing about the landing in Cuba, Walker wrote, "Meantime, with the transports at anchor four to six miles off shore, the animals—horses reserved for top officers and staff, orderlies and messengers, and mules for hauling transport wagons, and ambulances—were landed by the simple expediency of opening cargo ports, lowering the animals to the sea in slings, or by pushing them into the water, for them to swim to shore. Many of the terrified animals swam in the wrong direction toward Haiti and drowned." But while Roosevelt's big roan, "Little Texas," swam bravely and miraculously made it safely to the Daiquiri beach, his other horse,

"Rain-in-the-Face," purchased in San Antonio, was lowered from the horse transport by bellyband just as a huge wave smacked the ship and carried the horse to its death.

The *Handbook of Texas* states in its history of the Texas-trained "Rough Riders": "The Rough Riders catapulted Theodore Roosevelt into the vice presidency, and later the presidency of the United States." So Theodore Roosevelt, after training in big Texas, and mounted on "Little Texas," rode into the American spotlight and into the White House.

THE EYES OF TEXAS AND ROBERT E. LEE

At least partial credit for the official University of Texas song, "The Eyes of Texas," is due to famed Confederate General Robert E. Lee. The general, in addressing the graduating class at Washington College in Virginia, closed by reminding the graduating class that "The eyes of the South are upon you." A member of that class, William Prather, became president of the University of Texas. General Lee's stirring speech so impacted Mr. Prather that when he addressed U.T. graduates, he closed his address with "The eyes of Texas are upon you." The U.T. Glee Club composed a song for a minstrel show in 1903, spoofing Mr. Prather's admonition that the graduates were being watched. The song they presented was "The Eyes of Texas Are Upon You." When Mr. Prather died, the song was, at the widow's request, sung at the funeral.

EARLY TEXAS RAILROAD TUNNELS SERVED THE SOUTH PLAINS

The Fort Worth & Denver South Plains Railway Company was chartered March 6, 1925 to meet the competition of the Santa Fe, which was building into the cotton-rich South Plains out of Lubbock as a hub. By June 1927 this road had been completed 43 miles westward from Estelline, once the world's largest cattle shipping point. The 204-mile triple-pronged stretch into the South Plains embraces some of the most scenic country in Texas. The line boasts two tunnels, one 790 feet in length and the other 390 feet long, and makes fourteen six-degree curves in one ten-mile stretch through the Tule Canyon country near the Briscoe County town of Quitaque (pronounced kit uh kway). The roadbed, including one tunnel, is now a bike and hike trail through the scenic Caprock Canyon. The tunnel is a roost for thousands of Mexican free-tailed bats.

THE 1900 NEW YORK MURDER MYSTERY THAT BECAME A TEXAS LEGEND

Records inform the casual reader that one of Texas's most prestigious schools of higher learning, Rice University, was chartered in 1891 with a small endowment from William Marsh Rice, a successful merchant and industrialist. The school was opened for instruction in 1912, further endowed by the bulk of the Rice estate. What the record does not reveal at first glance is that had it not been for an alert New York banker, there might not have been a Rice University.

The school's benefactor died, practically a recluse, in his New York apartment in September 1900. At first the death of the doddering eighty-four-year-old man was believed to have been from natural causes. This was so stated by his regular physician, Dr. Walter Curry. A close review of contemporary newspapers, however, particularly the *New York Journal*, furnished to us by the archives of Rice University, reveals a tangled story of "fraud, forgery, falsehoods and murder," at the hands of two of Rice's closest confidants: his valet and personal secretary, Charles F. Jones, who, the paper says, "kept Rice a prisoner in his own home"; and Albert T. Patrick, his New York attorney.

The old newspaper reveals that Mr. Rice had been ill, suffering the simple complaints and symptoms experienced by many octogenarians. "He was," according to the *Journal*, "under the care of Dr. Curry, who was procured by lawyer Patrick." All of his nursing was done by his constant companion, Mr. Jones. The doctor, it seems, had prescribed a medicine which, when administered in small, proper doses, was perfectly safe, but in larger amounts could be lethally poisonous! His valet, Mr. Jones, dispensed the medication. Attorney Patrick presented a check in the amount of $25,000.00, made payable to him and signed by Mr. Rice, to Mr. Rice's bank for cashing. Finding the writing on the check "a little funny," the banker called to have the check approved by Mr. Rice. "Valet Jones," the *Journal* explained, "answered the phone and told the banker to cash the check, that it was good. The banker said that if Mr. Rice would tell him that on the wire, he would cash the check." The valet said, according to the news story, "Mr. Rice is deaf and cannot talk on the phone." When further pressed, the valet said Rice was asleep, and he "didn't want to awaken him." When the banker told the valet that he wouldn't cash the check for the attorney unless he spoke with Mr. Rice, it was then the valet told him Mr. Rice was dead.

All this mystique around the check caused an investigation to be set in motion. It was revealed that the team of valet Jones and lawyer Patrick had caused many thousands of dollars in cash and other assets to flow into their hands. Mr. Rice's will had even been changed to ensure that the bulk of Rice's estate, which was scheduled to endow Rice Institute, would go to Rice's trusted attorney, Patrick.

An autopsy was held by the New York coroner. This autopsy proved to be very difficult, as Mr. Rice's body had been so heavily embalmed as to be nearly mummified. This was done at the attorney's request, although the attorney knew that Mr. Rice, upon his death, was to have been cremated and did not require embalming. Embalming makes it most difficult to determine if some poisons are the cause of death! The two confidants were arrested and charged with forgery.

A *Dallas Morning News* article dated November 18, 1954 carries a story headlined as follows: "Key Figure in Classic Crime of 1900 Keeps Suicide Vow." Bearing a dateline of Houston, Texas, the article informs us that "an old man who had committed one of the classic crimes of the century, the murder of the founder of Rice Institute, has carried out a vow to kill himself. Charles F. Jones, was found shot to death Tuesday in his modest Baytown home." The article reminds us that Jones, although never convicted, had admitted the September 23, 1900 chloroform murder of William Marsh Rice, the eighty-four-year-old founder of the rich Houston school, in a swank New York City apartment. "Jones was charged with murder but went free after turning state's evidence against a codefendant Albert T. Patrick, an attorney and confidential advisor to Rice." According to the news account, Patrick was sentenced to death on conviction on charges that he forged Rice's will, named himself the residuary legatee of the estate, and talked Jones into killing his elderly employer. Patrick remained on Sing Sing's death row for four years before his sentence was commuted to life. In 1912 he obtained a full pardon. He died in Tulsa, Oklahoma in 1940 at age seventy-four.

In Martin L. Friedland's book, *The Death of Old Man Rice*, the author tells us that "Jones, in his mid-twenties, stepped forward with what seems an incredible confession. Under oath he swore that at Patrick's direction, he had placed a cone-shaped towel impregnated with chloroform over Rice's face as the old man lay sleeping and then had run from the room. When he returned a half hour later his victim was dead." Friedman, seemingly brushing this confession aside, tells his readers in another passage, "Sometime during the afternoon or evening of Sunday, September 23, 1900, William Marsh Rice died or was murdered in his apartment in New York City. He was well past 84 and had recently been in poor health." We can only comment that all the principal players in this murder mystery are dead. Only the university remains.

A BIT OF LORE GUARANTEED TO GIVE ALL TEXANS A LIFT

My mailbag yielded a bit of early Texas lore that proves that legends and lore do not have to be about the Texas Revolution and its revered heroes to be worthy of preservation, and sharing with the reading public, especially if it is guaranteed to give you a lift! This lore proves you can't keep a Texan down! The informative and very welcome letter was from Gregory J. Krauter, a director of the Kendall County Historical Commission. Mr. Krauter, who resides in the picturesque and historical Hill Country town of Comfort, provided a wealth of information about the nineteenth-century use of a mechanical marvel that we twenty-first-century Texans take for granted, elevators. Not just any elevators, mind you, but the "granddaddies" of all Texas elevators. These Comfort, Texas elevators have assisted Texans through their "ups and downs" for the better portion of a hundred years! Mr. Krauter's hometown is no stranger to nineteenth-century elevators. An Otis brand elevator was, according to its original identification plates, manufactured in Houston, Texas, and installed in 1907 in the Faltin General Store building, which was built in Comfort in 1879. The structure was one of a half dozen buildings in this town that were designed by the transplanted English architect, Alfred Giles.

The *Handbook of Texas* informs us that Giles came to the United States from London, England in 1872, and in 1875 he established the firm of Alfred Giles, Architect, in San Antonio, Texas. Giles owned about 13,000 acres of land near Comfort, Texas, where he raised horses and cattle. Mr. Krauter writes that the limestone block structure in which the elevator was installed replaced the single-story wood building built by the Goldbeck brothers in 1854, the year that Ernst Altgeld led a small body of settlers from New Braunfels and established the town of Comfort, which was originally called Camp Comfort.

The building was purchased in 1856 by August Friedrich Faltin, who was Mr. Krauter's great-great-grandfather. The elevator consisted of wooden planks on a metal frame; it traveled between the ground floor and the basement. The General Store closed in 1960. Some major components of the elevator were removed before the building closed, including the large pulley wheel and counterweights. August Faltin III, who operates an antique store in this historic building, told the author that before the eighty-eight-year-old elevator was installed, merchandise had to be unloaded from freight wagons by laying planks from the wagons to the cellar and rolling barrels or sliding boxes down the planks into the cellar. Mr. Faltin said that as a child he rode the elevator up and down amid the packing cases and boxes. The Otis was gravity operated using counterweights.

Mr. Krauter writes that a new elevator constructed entirely of wood was constructed in the new two-story, cut limestone Ingenhuett General Store building in 1880. This building was also designed by Alfred Giles. The elevator was made by Sydney Elevator Manufacturing Company of Sydney, Illinois. It traveled between the basement and second story (living quarters). The elevator was converted to electricity during remodeling of the building in 1948. Mr. Krauter tells us that Ingenhuett General Store is the oldest continually operating general store in the state of Texas. It is now being operated by the fifth generation, and the vintage elevator is still in use, though not by the public.

Although Comfort offers Texas history buffs more than an average amount of tangible evidence of how early Texas settlers lived, it is easy to overlook these "ahead-of-their-time" mechanical wonders, the nineteenth-century elevators that helped introduce these hardy pioneers to the machine age. We thank Mr. Krauter for his considerable contribution to our ever-growing collection of Texas trivia. The story of the elevators of Comfort is the kind of family lore that is so vital to painting a complete portrait of the developing land called TEXAS.

SHERMAN'S DAY OF LAWLESS SHAME

This heading is the way the *History of Grayson County, Texas,* published by Grayson County Frontier Village, Inc. in 1981, headlines an entry about a 1930 tragedy that is still talked about by some old-timers. Not unlike the notoriety Dallas inherited when President Kennedy was assassinated in that city, the article bemoans the fact that when Sherman is mentioned, folks are likely to say, "Isn't that the town where the courthouse was burned?" That may have been the case during the decade of the 1930s, but in my lifetime I've never even heard the story of Sherman's costly and deadly race riot of 1930. I would not have known had not the Frontier Village folks permitted me to peruse their county's history and use any excerpts I found that might enhance this book. This headline piqued my interest enough I thought the story merited exploring and passing on.

The essence of the incident was that a mob, which gathered for the trial of a black man accused of assaulting a white woman, became incensed when it was refused custody of the man. According to the *History of Grayson County*: "In the frenzied atmosphere of the mob, rocks were thrown through some windows of the courthouse and fire broke out when gasoline was hurled inside. The courthouse burned all night, as the crowd thwarted attempts of the fire department to extinguish the blaze, by slashing hoses with knives." The defendant had been placed in a steel vault for his own protection, and was presumed roasted to death in the blaze. About midnight leaders of the mob recovered the body after dynamiting the vault. Later indications were he survived the fire, but was killed by the dynamite blast. His body was dragged through the black section of town and hanged from a tree, under which a fire was built. An estimated $75,000 damage was done to the black business district in the night of destruction. "The night of terror had three visible effects," says the *History of Grayson County:* "1. The loss of human life of George Hughes, 2. The destruction of the Grayson County courthouse, and 3. The destruction of valuable and historic documents of Grayson County."

THE STOLEN KISS THAT STARTED A FOOD EMPIRE

The eighty-three-year-old mind of Royce Hailey was still sharp as the proverbial tack when I interviewed him at a retirement home in Mesquite, Texas, and that mind remained sharp right up until his death on November 1, 2000. His memory was particularly vivid on one incident that occurred seventy years before. When I interviewed the onetime owner of a Dallas dining institution, the Pig Stand restaurants, he related to me how a stolen kiss acted as a stepping-stone to the presidency of the legendary dining chain, and subsequently its ownership.

Mr. Hailey said that at age thirteen he had attempted to get a job at the Pig Stand in the Trinity Heights section of Dallas's Oak Cliff. The manager said he was too young to work, even though young Hailey only wanted to be a carhop. Mr. Hailey said he continued to pester the manager about working until one day, September 15, 1930, to be exact, the manager said to him, "See that girl sitting on the porch swing across the street?" Not knowing what that had to do with getting a job, young Hailey said he

This 1929 photo shows the Pig Stand in the Trinity Heights section of Dallas where thirteen-year-old Royce Hailey went to work as a carhop after stealing a kiss from a young neighbor girl. The young entrepreneur (now deceased) is the fourth young man from the left, kneeling in the front row. Mr. Hailey's son, Richard, followed in his father's footsteps—but not in stealing kisses! He now successfully operates several Pig Stands in South Texas. We are grateful to him for furnishing this photo.

did. The manager told him, "If you will go and kiss that girl, I'll give you a job." Mr. Hailey told me how he walked across the street and told the girl exactly why he was going to kiss her. "I think she just wanted to help me," Hailey said. "She didn't voice any objection, so I planted one on her!" The kiss resulted in Royce Hailey landing a job as a carhop. The shocked girl's kiss did more than just land Hailey a job. It launched a Horatio Alger-like career. Young Royce would later become owner of Pig Stands Inc. and served as its corporate president.

Royce Hailey is also credited with inventing the popular "Texas toast." He told us that honors for creating the popular Texas toast had to be shared with one of his cooks in a Beaumont Pig

Stand, when he was manager of the diners in that city. "The discovery was quite by accident," confessed Hailey. "It was Christmas and Rainbo Bakery delivered part of my bread order unsliced. I had to slice the bread by hand. I cut some of the slices too thick and they wouldn't fit in my toaster. My cook suggested we butter the bread on both sides and toast them on the grill. The grill-toasted slices came out soft on the inside and crunchy on the crust. The customers liked the new creation and began to order the thick toast, which I added to the menu as 'Toast as big as the Lone Star State.' " As the Texas-size toast grew in popularity, it was copied by other restaurants.

HOOVER HOGS OF TEXAS

In the Great Depression years of the 1930s many East Texans, because of a lack of ready cash, began to eat armadillos. While plentiful in Texas, this animal is not considered game to be eaten by most. These animals came to be referred to locally as Hoover hogs, not because their meat tasted like pork, but as a sarcastic slap at U.S. president Herbert Hoover, whom many blamed for the Depression.

THE RED RIVER WAR

The Red River bridge controversy, sometimes referred to as the "Red River War," which pitted the governor and citizens of Texas against the governor and residents of Oklahoma, occurred in July 1931, over the opening of a free bridge built jointly by both states between Denison, Texas and Durant, Oklahoma.

The Red River Bridge Company, a private firm that operated an already established toll bridge that paralleled the free bridge, attempted to prevent the opening of the new free bridge. The company claimed that the Highway Commission had earlier agreed to purchase the toll bridge for $60,000. A temporary injunction was issued and Texas governor Ross Sterling ordered barricades erected across the approaches to the new bridge. Oklahoma governor William "Alfalfa Bill" Murray opened the bridge by executive

The author with his nine-banded armadillo, "Lil' Tex." These animals are the official small mammal of Texas. Surprisingly they were prized for their meat during the Great Depression. Known then as "Hoover hogs," they are best known today as roadkill. Photo from author's collection.

order, claiming that Oklahoma's half of the bridge ran north and south across the Red River, which Oklahoma had title to as a result of the Louisiana Purchase Treaty of 1803. Texas governor Sterling ordered a detachment of three Texas Rangers, accompanied by Adjutant General William Sterling, to rebuild the barricades torn down on orders of the Oklahoma governor. The Oklahoma governor ordered Oklahoma highway crews to tear up the northern approaches to the still-operating toll bridge, and ordered traffic over the bridge to halt. Mass meetings were held in Denison and Sherman demanding the opening of the free bridge. In special session the Texas Legislature passed a bill granting the Red River Bridge Company the right to sue the state of Texas to recover the sum they claimed was owed them. On July 25th the free bridge was open to traffic and the Rangers were withdrawn. In a Federal Court in Oklahoma Governor Murray was enjoined from blocking the northern entrance to the toll bridge.

However, the Oklahoma governor still had a card to play in the bridge war! The governor declared martial law in a narrow strip along the northern approaches to both bridges. He argued that, as commander in chief of the Oklahoma National Guard, he was above the federal act. Murray ordered the National Guard to the bridge and, according to some published reports, Murray showed up at the bridge with an antique revolver, making a personal appearance at the "war zone," as some newspapers branded it.

EVIDENCE POINTS TO TEXAS DECLARATION OF INDEPENDENCE BEING WRITTEN IN TENNESSEE!

George C. Childress, for whom the city and county are named, is credited with being the author of the Texas Declaration of Independence. Childress was a lawyer and newspaper editor from Nashville, Tennessee. Before moving to Texas he supported the cause of the Texians, and after his arrival in Texas, he was appointed a delegate to the convention of 1836. There Childress was made chairman of a committee to draft a Declaration of Independence for Texas. The *Handbook of Texas* tells us that "it is generally conceded that Childress wrote the instrument with little help from the others. There is some evidence that he brought to the convention a proposed declaration that was adopted with little change by the committee and the convention, a view which is substantiated by the fact that the committee was appointed on March 1 and the declaration was presented to the convention on March 2." This would bear out the belief of some that the Declaration was written by Childress in Tennessee and brought with him.

THE LEGEND OF DALLAS'S TEXAS THEATER REACHES BEYOND KENNEDY ASSASSINATION

The old cliché "A legend in its own time" is a description that fits Dallas's Texas Theater like a kid glove. This theater is not only the venue where the alleged assassin of John F. Kennedy, Lee Harvey Oswald, was wrestled into submission by Dallas police after the president's shooting, and after Oswald murdered Dallas police officer J. D. Tippit. This movie house, which was built in 1931, has other historic credits. The Texas was the first Dallas theater designed especially for talking motion pictures. It was also the city's first air-conditioned theater.

HAVE YOU EVER WONDERED WHY THE LONE RANGER WEARS A MASK?

If you, like most of us who grew up listening to and watching the adventures of the Lone Ranger, have wondered why this defender of justice wears a mask, this legend is for you! Yes! This peculiar trait of a fictional character has enough of a Texas connection to warrant it being included in our woven fabric of Texas legends. While our collection of Texas trivia is based on fact and timeworn lore, this fragment from a fertile imagination has, as its basis, one of Texas's beloved icons, the Texas Rangers. Thus it warrants special consideration and inclusion.

Our reference material on early radio shows tells us that in 1930, George Trindle, while searching for a radio script that he could submit as a possible radio show about the Old West,

Dallas's historic Texas Theater is probably best known as the site of the capture of accused assassin of President John F. Kennedy, Lee Harvey Oswald. The theater, which is currently being remodeled, is of other historical significance to the city. Photo by Marianne Cannon.

invented a character who was a Texas Ranger by the name of John Reid. One of the early story lines finds Ranger Reid and his troop of five Rangers engaged in a blazing gun battle with the Butch Cavendish gang. The reference tells us that all the Rangers were killed save Reid. The lone remaining Ranger observes to his Indian friend, Tonto, that "if the evil gang realizes that one Ranger survived, they would hunt him down and kill him." Tonto replied, "Them no think you survive, me bury five dead Rangers, but make six graves." Reid now becomes "The Lone Ranger." Reid realizes that the Cavendishes know him by sight and his life will always be in danger. Reid tells Tonto that he must create a disguise or wear a mask. "Yes, that's it, I'll wear a mask." So as long as the Lone Ranger might be in danger of recognition, he must wear the mask that has become so familiar to all of us.

According to that first story line, John Reid's mask was especially meaningful to him. One of the five Rangers killed in Reid's troop that fateful day was Reid's youngest brother. When the Rangers were laid to rest, Reid removed his brother's black leather vest. It was from this link to his brave dead brother, so the story goes, that Ranger John Reid carefully and poignantly cut his now famous mask.

TEXAS A&M'S BLAZING OUTHOUSES

In an interview at the Christian Care Center with the late Robert Norwood, who was a freshman at Texas A&M University in 1931, he shared with me some insight into the university's traditional bonfires, constructed and torched for each of the school's football games with rival Texas University. Mr. Norwood told us that while the bonfires were constructed of all manner of scrap lumber, one component that was traditionally included was an outhouse with the initials U.T. painted on it. The privies, which had been purloined from neighboring towns and communities, topped out the bonfire like some earthy Christmas angel, or star, said Mr. Norwood. We asked Bob when the outhouse tradition stopped. Bob smugly replied that it stopped when all of the available outhouses had been absconded with.

SYMPATHY FOR STUDENT SAVED A&M TRADITION

Bob Norwood also said that when he entered Texas A&M in 1931, the hazing of freshmen was a tradition of long standing. "Christmas licks" with a wooden paddle was a painful, but cherished tradition. Bob explained that each year prior to Christmas, each freshman made his own wooden paddle. On Christmas the freshman took his hazing weapon to each upperclassman, who was expected to administer one lick to the freshman's buttocks. This accomplished, the upperclassman signed the paddle, signifying that he had administered the customary lick.

When Bob was commander of his cadet company, one freshman from Throckmorton, Texas flunked out at Thanksgiving and, although he wouldn't be returning as a student, he had enough pride and school spirit to make a "hazing paddle" and return at Christmastime for his "Christmas licks." The student brought the paddle to Bob first, as he was his company commander. Bob dutifully administered his Christmas licks and signed the former student's paddle. The boy's father was upset when he found the boy's hazing paddle and went to a former classmate, who went to Colonel Anderson, the commandant of the Corps. The commandant announced that Bob would no longer command his company and demoted all upperclassmen to sergeant. He also announced that hazing would be no more. In support of Norwood, all company commanders removed their rank insignias and resigned command of their companies. The hazing furor was so intense that the commandant inspected the buttocks of all freshmen, and finding not a mark, reinstated Norwood and the hazing tradition.

TEXAS A&M'S MASCOT, REVEILLE

When Bob Norwood was an A&M freshman, students were not allowed to have automobiles on campus. Bob told us that often the students would take the bus to Bryan to see a movie. On one such occasion, he saw a dog wet from drizzling rain shivering by the side of the road. Mr. Norwood said that he took the dog back to his dormitory, where he was given a warm bath and dried. The next morning, Bob said, as was the custom, the cadets marched to breakfast in formation, led by the A&M band. When the stray dog heard the band start to play, he bolted from the dorm and ran directly to the band. The band adopted the dog and named him Reveille. This stray dog became the first in a long line of Reveilles to be A&M's mascot. Those collies who were Reveilles, and who have since died, are buried near Kyle Field. The late Bob Norwood lays claim to finding A&M's first Reveille.

ADOLF HITLER UNWITTINGLY HELPED FURNISH LABOR FORCE FOR CONSTRUCTION OF LAKE TEXOMA

Although a construction project in America was not a part of their original plans, some of Hitler's crack panzer (tank) troops were involved in the initial construction efforts of Red River Dam at Denison that created Lake Texoma. These men, who made up some of Hitler's top fighting forces before their capture in North Africa, were brought from their POW camps to Denison in spring 1943 and were responsible for helping get this massive construction project started by felling the trees on 300,000 acres of land. Although this was denied in official U.S. government circles, there were German citizens living in America when the war started on December 7, 1941 who were picked up by the U.S. government and held in internment camps, and who also were sent to Denison to work on the mammoth construction site. A personal friend in the German community in Dallas told us how her father was picked up in Fort Worth and sent to an internment camp in the Dakotas. He was subsequently transferred to a camp in Oklahoma, and then assigned to work on the Red River Dam.

HITLER TAKES ADVANTAGE OF TEXAS-OKLAHOMA DISPUTE

During the so-called "Red River War" Hitler's propagandists ran a photo of heavily armed Oklahoma National Guard troops patrolling the north end of the disputed toll bridge after Texas

Rangers restored the court-ordered barricades at the Texas end of the free span in a Nazi magazine as proof that a state of civil war existed in the United States.

BIG INCH AND LITTLE BIG INCH

During World War II Secretary of the Interior Harold Ickes recognized the threat posed by German U-boats against oil tankers attempting to transport petroleum products from Texas to the northern and eastern states by way of the eastern seaboard. In order to supply these states with petroleum products, he was responsible for two pipelines to be laid from the East Texas oil field to the northeastern regions. These pipelines became known as the "Big Inch" and the "Little Big Inch." The Big Inch was twenty-four inches in diameter and the Little Big Inch was twenty inches in diameter. A ditch four feet deep, three feet wide, and 1,254 miles long was dug to accommodate the two pipelines. The ditch was dug from Longview, Texas across the Mississippi River to south Illinois, and then to Phoenixville, Pennsylvania, with twenty-inch lines from there to New York City and Philadelphia. The cost of the two pipelines was $146 million.

COCHRAN'S CONVENT

Cochran's Convent, located in Sweetwater, Texas, was not a religious order but the nickname given to Avenger Field, home to the only all-women training air base in the history of flying. During World War II (1943–44), 2,500 women applied for duty in the Women's Air Force Service Pilots (or WASP) Corps. Only 1,074 passed the screening tests. These paid their own way to Sweetwater and entered training under the command of Jacqueline Cochran. Jacqueline saw to it that these trainees lived a regimented life and learned to fly the army way. These heroic women, whose job it was to ferry war planes to foreign shores, relieved combat flyers to battle America's enemies! Lots of male pilots made an effort to get on the base, but the rules were so strict that the training field soon became known as "Cochran's Convent."

"OLD BETSY" MAY NOT HAVE REACHED TEXAS

Where would Texana buffs like myself be without the likes of folks like my friend Kent Biffle, whose "Texana" column appears regularly in the *Dallas Morning News*. Kent's spicy meanderings through the history and colorful footnotes of Texas history have, over the years, served to inspired me to leap, magnifying glass in hand, into the pages of Texas history, as well as examine closely the "she said/he said" remembrances offered as folklore by like-minded, and well-meaning, sages bent on keeping every tidbit of Texana alive and well! Kent's column of July 7, 2002 was just another example of the nuggets of precious Texas trivia that, as Kent would expect, set my investigative juices flowing in search of "just one more crumb" to jealously guard in my mental vault of Texas trivia that runs the gamut from "Gee! I've always wondered about that" to "Who gives a damn!"

In the column referred to, Kent writes that Davy Crockett's famous rifle, "Old Betsy," did not accompany the coonskin-chapeaued Tennessean to Texas when he came with his trusted friends to help Texas separate itself from the harsh terms of the Mexican Constitution of 1824. Kent referred to a letter from Don Cooper, editor of the Hereford, Texas *Brand*, in which Cooper contends that "Old Betsy" was presented to Crockett while he was a member of Congress. Mr. Cooper explains that "When the Crockett party stopped for a few days in Little Rock, Arkansas, Davy left 'Old Betsy' with friends, because 'Old Betsy' was a percussion-cap rifle. Crockett was afraid he might not be able to get the caps in Texas, so he took a flint-lock with him." "Old Betsy" was left in Arkansas and today is kept in a vault of the Old Statehouse Museum in Little Rock.

Considering that Davy Crockett and "Old Betsy" are so much a part of Texas lore, what better place to showcase this gem of Alamo trivia than in this book designed for exposure of just such forgotten and little-known facts about the Lone Star State? We are indebted to Don Cooper and Kent Biffle for enlightening us with this Alamo trivia. It is a bit like finding a Rembrandt showing up at a neighborhood garage sale. Thanks, guys!

But, and there is a But! Like most garage sale purchases, when examined under pure light, one may find a chink or two in the otherwise desirable treasure. Our investigation into the "Old Betsy" story revealed a flaw or two, none of which diminished this story's value. In fact, the discoveries led us on a pursuit of the elusive rifle, with unexpected rewards for this book! First, the curator at the Old Statehouse Museum in Little Rock could find no record of the famous Crockett rifle ever being in that museum, in the vault or elsewhere. We were directed to the Arkansas Historic Commission, which was, we were told, once housed in the Old Statehouse Museum. Luck smiled on us when we were introduced to Dr. John L. Ferguson, the Arkansas state historian. Dr. Ferguson's research into "Old Betsy" resulted in a letter informing us that "The Davy Crockett rifle was loaned to the Arkansas History Commission on Dec. 23, 1915 by John Wesley Crockett (1860–1920), a great grandson of David Crockett. John Wesley Crockett, a former State Treasurer and Secretary of State, was the son of Robert Hamilton Crockett (1832–1902), who came to Arkansas from Paris, Henry County, Tennessee in 1856." Dr. Ferguson went on to say that the rifle was reclaimed on July 1, 1951 by the widow of John W. Crockett. A copy of the original receipt and return notation by Dr. Dallas T. Herndon, director of the Arkansas History Commission from 1912 until 1953, as well as a photo of the famous rifle, was generously provided by Dr. Ferguson. Interestingly, on the return receipt, the article is shown as "Rifle, one time property of the hon. David Crockett." We are grateful to Dr. Ferguson and the Arkansas History Commission for making this information and material available for use in our book. Like all good mysteries, some questions remain unanswered. We know that "Old Betsy" was not in an Arkansas museum at the time of Crockett's defense of the Alamo. But whether or not he left it in the possession of his family when he continued on to Texas after stopping in Arkansas is not known.

1996 WAS A BANNER YEAR FOR TEXAS (A STAR-SPANGLED BANNER YEAR, THAT IS!)

As is the case with all passing of time, it is nearly impossible to imagine a time when Texas was not a part of the "upper 48." Most of us who call ourselves Texans have little trouble conjuring up in our minds the vivid details of the heroic struggle waged by our forefathers in their fight to free Tejas from Mexico to form the Republic of Texas. Sometimes it takes a birthday or anniversary to jar us back to the reality that we were not always the state of Texas. Such was the case in February of 1996 when we celebrated the sesquicentennial of our statehood.

In a Texas Trivia column we wrote during that month, for a local weekly newspaper, *The Metro News*, we pointed out a number of facts that could easily qualify as "Forgotten footnotes to our Texas history." In our column we mentioned that "while some will be quick to point out that Texas's legal entry into the union was, according to the *Handbook of Texas*, December 29, 1845, the date on which the state constitution was accepted by the United States Congress, we counter that the transfer of authority from the Republic to the state was not made until February 19, 1846. We must add that the United States Postal Service issued commemorative stamps for Texas statehood in 1945 and 1995." Our column was not designed as a forum for teaching Texas history, but to let the light of day shine on those unusual facts of our history and the culture of its people. These unusual facts are what we call trivia. This important phase of our history is not without its morsels of trivia, which we believe are worth recalling.

CHARGÉ D'AFFAIRES ISAAC VAN ZANDT Perhaps the difference in being Texas, the state, and Texas, the republic, is no better pointed out than by the fact that Texas once had a chargé d'affaires assigned to Washington D.C. in the United States. The accepted definition of a chargé d'affaires is a representative of one country to a foreign country to conduct the affairs of his nation. In 1842 Sam Houston appointed Isaac Van Zandt, a Marshall lawyer, as chargé d'affaires to the United States. The county of Van

Zandt is named for him. Van Zandt played an active role in the Republic's bid for statehood. Great Britain opposed Texas statehood. One footnote in the history of Texas's efforts toward statehood is the fact that one foreign power wanted to prevent Texas's annexation into the United States. According to the *Handbook of Texas*, Great Britain opposed annexation of Texas into the United States and even contemplated force to prevent it. It did not want to add Texas to the British Empire, but it wanted to prevent the westward expansion of the U.S., to reap the commercial advantages of Texas trade. Britain's policy over Texas so alarmed the U.S. that annexation of Texas, which had been rejected, was rushed through. Annexation was completed December 29, 1845.

THE FIVE STATES OF TEXAS Unusual as it seems, it is a possibility! This is another of those facts that are a forgotten footnote to Texas history. The resolution adopted by Congress allowing the annexation of Texas had the provision that Texas "could be divided into states of convenient size, not to exceed four, in addition to the said state of Texas." Which, according to the wording could allow five states. Our column concluded by asserting that such a division of Texas was doubtful, as each division would surely insist on having a part of the Alamo, which is an impossibility.

Chapter Two

TEXAS IS PEOPLE

Its vastness, the beauty of its diverse landscapes, the untold richness of its natural resources, its dramatic history, including the thirteen days of glory at the Alamo, are all just individual brush strokes that blend together to make this world-renowned masterpiece known as Texas. But none of these, dynamic as they are, can measure up to the state's major resource that truly makes Texas **TEXAS!**: its people.

Nearly every elementary schoolchild can recite the names of the heroes of the Texas Revolution; their names are engraved on the facades of school buildings, printed on street signs, and are just as deeply etched into the hearts and minds of Texans from all walks of life. But these are not the only names that have elevated Texas to its lofty position of preeminence in the world. The Anglo settlers who settled in the Spanish Province of Tejas y Coahuila were men and women of resolve and courage. Many came allured by the offer of cheap land and the idea of self-determination in a brand new land. When they had their land, they sank their roots deep into the precious, rich-smelling soil. When men tried to rip them from their hard-won soil, they dug their collective heels in the Texas earth and, with a bold daring, routed their would-be tormentors, who had severely underestimated what was later to become known as "the Spirit of Texas."

These were the common folk of Texas—common folk with an uncommon determination to make a fresh start in an inhospitable land. These were the fathers who were to sire a nation/state of thinkers and doers unmatched, we believe, anywhere else on God's sphere called Earth. These were the proud Texians who would, after surviving some of the most brutal battles on record, and after much political haranguing, be called **TEXANS!** In this section of *Texas: Land of Legend and Lore*, we present a few of the Texans who typify the contributions made by the common folk of Texas, as well as some non-Texans who used the Lone Star State as a backdrop for their claim to fame. In this section we salute all Texans! Each with his individual pride in and love of state has added his individual contribution toward creating the Texas mystique, some more dramatically than others; but each in his own way has made Texas great!

TWO CENTURIES OF TEXANS WHO WORE BLACK HATS!

As we said in our introduction to this segment of the book, it took all kinds of people to settle and develop the Lone Star State. This is because from the day Texas stopped being Tejas, and became Texas, it was a whole 'nuther country! There are legends, and then there are legends! While Texas heroes are abundant, and most can be named by most elementary schoolchildren, the state also has sired an ample supply of the infamous, who, in the parlance of Hollywood's Western movies, *wore black hats.* Saying "sired" might be a bit too fault-finding of our state, as some of the desperados, banditos, and pistoleros drifted across our state's borders from neighboring states like Missouri, Arkansas, and Oklahoma. They were, as the "Boll Weevil Song" says, "just a lookin' for a home." And Texas in the mid-1800s was a pretty safe choice, being practically lawless and all that!

One of the Southwest's most notorious dime novel subjects, Billy the Kid, even came from New York City! Can you imagine that, a Yankee desperado? Mugger, yes, but desperado? But the glorious pages of Texas history are stained by legends of enough badmen to fill a good-sized Boot Hill. Its only fair to them and to our readers to open the state's closet door a crack and let in just enough light to expose a few of the skeletons of those who, during the Wild West days of the 1800s and even the twentieth century, have made Texas more exciting than some Texas lawmen cared to cope with! Perhaps a look back through the rogues' gallery of early Texas will satiate our collective morbid curiosities about the bloodletters and badmen and -women of Texas. Not all wearers of the black hat spent their leisure time whittling notches on the handles of their Colt revolvers, or wiping the bloodstains from their equalizer of choice before the advent of the Colt: the Bowie knife. Sissified as it sounds, "white collar" crime was also a part of the early Texas mystique!

MONROE EDWARDS Monroe earned a space in the *Handbook of Texas*, which called him "Smuggler and forger par excellence." Edwards came to Texas in 1827. He became engaged in smuggling slaves from Cuba to Texas. His first venture brought him $50,000, with which he bought land in Brazoria County, which he called Chenengo Plantation. Plantation life was too unexciting for Edwards. In partnership with Christopher Dart he continued smuggling slaves. After several swindles, which spanned the Atlantic from the East Coast to Europe, Edwards was apprehended in Philadelphia and tried in New York, where he was sentenced to Sing Sing prison. He died in 1847 after being severely whipped by prison authorities for attempted escape.

SYDNEY PORTER Another transplanted Texan who was catapulted into fame and fortune as a result of his nonviolent style of white collar crime may come as a slight surprise. Sydney Porter, who came to Texas by way of North Carolina, was a magazine publisher in Austin between 1894 and 1895. Porter was arrested in 1898 for embezzling funds from a bank where he worked as a teller. It was while in prison in Columbus, Ohio, that Porter began writing short stories, many of which had a Texas setting. This Austin embezzler sold his writing under the pseudonym of "O. Henry": and the rest is literary history!

SAM BASS Stages and trains were favorite targets of bandits like Sam Bass. This miscreant, originally from Indiana, worked as a teamster around Denton, Texas. History records show that he went north to Nebraska with a trail drive. He fell in with a group of outlaws. After the owlhoots robbed a Union Pacific train in the fall of 1877, Bass returned to North Texas. He planned to rob a bank in Round Rock, Texas, just north of Austin, in 1878, but one of the gang members alerted the Texas Rangers. When the Bass gang rode into Round Rock on June 19th, Rangers confronted them. In the ensuing gunfire, Bass was mortally wounded. Bass was only in Texas about eight years, and on the run less than a year when killed at Round Rock. A not so easily verified piece of Bass trivia is a story that says although the infamous outlaw was, indeed, mortally wounded in the thwarted bank robbery, his body does not lie in the grave visited by many tourists attracted to Round Rock.

THE BADMAN WHO BURIED HIS VICTIM Clay Allison, who achieved renown as a gunfighter in the Southwest in the 1870s and 1880s, spent time in North Texas because he had a ranch in the Texas Panhandle near Mobeetie. He became known as "Clay Allison of the Washita." He appeared in Colfax County, New Mexico, supposedly after a strange duel with Bowie knives in a roomy grave dug by Allison and his opponent. The winner was to shovel dirt over the loser. Allison did the shoveling. In a book about Allison's life by Maurice Fulton, it was written that after a life of lead-slinging, including facing such notables as Bat Masterson and Wyatt Earp, Allison met his death when he fell from a loaded wagon and was crushed beneath its wheels.

BELIEVE IT OR NOT! One Texas outlaw actually held the title of "Queen." The title was, I think you'll agree, not so regal! Belle Starr was born Myrabelle Shirley in 1848 in Missouri. At the end of the Civil War, the family moved to Scyene, Texas east of Dallas. She eloped with a horse thief, Jim Reed, from Missouri. Reed, who was also a stagecoach bandit, was wanted in connection with several killings. Reed was killed resisting arrest in 1874. The next few years the widow did some roving around, and she was accused of disposing of some livestock stolen by her male friends. In 1880 she went to the Indian Territory and married a Cherokee Indian by the name of Sam Starr. Their place became headquarters for a band of ruffians. In 1883 both Sam and Belle were convicted of horse theft and sent to prison. It was, no doubt, Belle's nefarious activities in what is, today, Oklahoma that won her the less-than-honorable title of "Outlaw Queen of the Indian Territory." Belle Starr was killed by an unknown gunman near her house in 1889.

THE BARROW GANG Perhaps still fresh in the minds of many Texans today are the exploits of the notorious Clyde Barrow and his Rowena- and West Dallas-bred, poem-writing moll, Bonnie Parker. Clyde Chesnut Barrow of Dallas and the shotgun-wielding Parker woman were the core of the infamous, headline-grabbing gang that led lawmen from several states on a two-year reign of terror that seemed much longer. Their robberies of banks and small businesses, and any other place whose till might still hold a few dollars to keep gasoline in their getaway car of choice—the Ford V8—during this era of the Great Depression, kept fear in the hearts of honest citizens across Texas and the Midwest. The newspapers chalked up at least a dozen murders to the pair's credit, two of the most senseless being the cold-blooded execution of two young motorcycle cops whose misfortune it was to happen upon the pair parked on a highway on the outskirts of Grapevine, Texas, and chose to investigate the suspicious car. A local farmer watched in horror from his front porch as first the man and then the woman brutally executed the young officers as they lay in the road. These and other terrorist acts earned them the unenviable title of "Public Enemy Number One." The pair laughed in the face of Texas Rangers and local police until one day in 1934, when they died together in a fusillade of police gunfire in a cleverly set up police ambush near Arcadia, Louisiana. The self-proclaimed "Robin Hoods" of the Depression era are both buried in the Dallas area. This police ambush brought a sigh of relief to lawmen and citizens alike!

THE BLACKEST OF BLACK HATS? Although he posed no threat to his contemporaries, of all the dubious distinctions one could claim, one man who lived in Texas claimed to wear the blackest hat of all! According to reports in the July 28, 1978 edition of the *Times Herald*, Granbury, Texas was home to a man calling himself John St. Helen who, prior to his death in 1903, confessed that he was President Lincoln's assassin, John Wilkes Booth. St. Helen moved to Texas five years after Lincoln's death. St. Helen had been a saloonkeeper in Granbury. Residents believed the man's claim, stating that he frequently quoted Shakespeare; and Booth was a noted Shakespearean actor. St. Helen's body was mummified and exhibited in traveling circuses, according to press releases. Adding to the mystery further is the reported fact that the body disappeared mysteriously in 1938.

CAPTAIN JAMES "BRIT" BAILEY (PRIDE TO THE EXTREME)

Call it eccentric, call it crazy, call it what you like, but, by his own words, James Briton "Brit" Bailey's strange deathbed wish was based on pure pride. This lesser luminary of Texas history illuminated one Texas characteristic in a strange way! Pride may be one of the seven deadly sins, but it is also one of the cardinal characteristics of many Texans, particularly those nineteenth-century Texians. Not many Texans carried their pride as far as "Brit" Bailey. Bailey was truly one of Texas's little-known luminaries. As often as I personally traveled the highway between my home in Houston and Brazoria to visit friends living on the San Bernard River, I never turned off to visit Bailey's Prairie, which would have enabled me to visit the unique grave of the community's namesake, Captain James "Brit" Bailey. Bailey came to Texas prior to Stephen F. Austin and settled near the Brazos River on what is today Bailey's Prairie. Brazoria County historians tell us that on his deathbed he told his wife that "He had never bowed or stooped to any man, nor had he ever been knocked down." He then requested that he be buried feet down so no man could ever look upon his grave and say, "There lays old 'Brit' Bailey, flat on his back." Honoring his request, upon his death in 1833, his wife had a vertical grave dug, and had Bailey's casket lowered into it feet first! Bailey's exaggerated pride was, no doubt, borne out of misplaced manliness.

BOUND FOR THE PROMISED LAND: TEXAS'S EARLY SETTLERS WORE A "COAT OF MANY COLORS"

Texas is people and one can hardly write about the people of Texas without including a sketch depicting those hardy pioneers who pulled up stakes in neighboring states and ventured out in search of what was often billed as, or at least implied to be, "The Promised Land." The allure of Texas, with its vast unspoiled land, drew settlers desperate to put down roots in fertile, affordable land. To thousands of Americans, and many foreign immigrants alike, this new land called Texas was truly the promised land. Larita Pierson, writing in the *Antique Almanac,* told the story of Texas's earliest settlers about as well as anyone I have read. She and *Antique Almanac* graciously gave us permission to use portions of her article, for which we are grateful. Ms. Pierson was specifically writing about the settling of that part of North Texas known to some as "Four Corners." This area of North Texas's blackest prairie is the juncture of Grayson, Fannin, Collin, and Hunt Counties.

This most interesting insight into the lives of these Texas pioneers, both good and bad, flows from Ms. Pierson's pen with exciting realism. "There's rich black soil just waiting for us to come and take it. Just across the Red in Texas. 'G.T.T.' across the doors of boarded up stores, closed down law offices, abandoned cabins, nailed to broken down buggies, or hung on rusted windmills. In Kentucky, Missouri, Mississippi, and Arkansas. All declared, 'Gone to Texas.' Earliest immigrants sought the promised 'League (4428.4 acres) and labor (177.136)' in Texas. They were told they could put their past behind them. They would be free. Virtually a law unto themselves, they no longer needed to worry about the debts and failures they were leaving behind. Their future was as rich, unexplored, as the land they were seeking. The land between the Red and Sabine was particularly considered a 'no man's land' beyond the authority of the U.S. Though technically a part of Mexico, its inaccessibility hampered the enforcement of that government's power. The area attracted the best and the worst. A seeming haven for thieves, cutthroats, and vagabonds. Only the boldest, strongest, and most determined individuals were ready to face the dangers for the promise offered. Even Texas' brightest stars came from a shadowy past. There were rumors that Bowie had killed a man in a duel. As we have written before, Houston left behind the governorship of Tennessee and a bride of a few weeks. Crockett couldn't seem to settle anywhere. Arriving before 1836, many joined the struggle for independence, while others like Andy Thomas of Kentuckytown, who, it is said traveled with Crockett, stayed to settle the land. The Kentuckytown settlement, the oldest in the area, is still known as 'Andy Thomas country.' The small Kentuckytown Cemetery seen from Highway 11 on a rise of land hosts the remains of heroes as well as scoundrels, a soldier of the Confederacy and a horse thief. It is a fitting example of the variety of pioneers who set the stage for the drama that was to unfold in the 'Four Corners.' Though with the coming of Texas Independence the nature of land grants had changed, immigration still continued through the Civil War and Reconstruction into the turn of the century, with settlers coming all across the U.S. and Europe. Yet, regardless of when they came, or where they came from, there was one common bond. The crossing of the Red River into the 'Promised Land.' The escape from iniquities, whether committed by them, or against them. Here in this raw, new land, untouched, unspoiled, unexplored, they could find freedom, put down roots, make a new start, grow with the land. Then as now, Texas was the land of opportunity. Their hearts high and full of hope, they sang as they walked or rode, 'We are bound for the promised Land.' " Texas is people, and these early settlers were truly a patchwork coat of many colors, as Larita Pierson has so graphically illustrated in her work, which she graciously permitted us to reproduce in part.

SAM HOUSTON'S DUAL CITIZENSHIP

Following his failed marriage, the details of which are shrouded in secrecy, and his resignation as governor of Tennessee, Sam Houston fled across the Mississippi into Indian Territory, where he established residency among the Cherokees. As a possible heir to Andrew Jackson, Houston may have given up the opportunity to become president of the United States. Houston was subsequently granted Cherokee citizenship in 1829. Under Cherokee law he married Diana, or Tiana, Rogers Gentry, an Indian woman of mixed blood. It has been written that "Houston denounced his American citizenship, and declared himself a citizen of the Cherokee Nation." We find no evidence to that effect; if he did not, Houston enjoyed dual citizenship at the time he lived with the Indians. One historian claims that Houston's new wife was the great-grand-aunt of Oklahoma humorist Will Rogers. Houston and Diana moved into Houston's log house, which he called "Wigwam Neosho," where they operated a trading post near Fort Gibson in present-day Oklahoma.

SUSANNA DICKINSON (THE BEARER OF ILL TIDINGS)

Susanna Dickinson, a native of Tennessee and a survivor of the siege of the Alamo, was married to Almaron Dickinson, who lost his life in the battle to defend the Alamo. After being discovered hiding in the old church, Mrs. Dickinson was released by Mexican General Santa Anna, who sent her with a letter of warning to Sam Houston. This twenty-two-year-old widow had the awesome responsibility of taking the sad news of the fall of the Alamo to Sam Houston. Susanna's two-year-old daughter, Angelina, around whose neck, according to legend, Alamo commander William Travis tied his cat's-eye ring, gained her own fame in the pages of Texas history as "The Babe of the Alamo."

SANTA ANNA'S LICENSE TO MURDER

Some Texas historians, in writing about Sam Houston's quick and decisive Battle of San Jacinto, have stated that many of Santa Anna's soldiers, facing annihilation at the hands of the rebellious Texians, could be heard screaming, "Me no Alamo! . . . Me no Goliad!" These guilt-ridden soldiers were loudly disavowing their complicity in the heinous murders of prisoners of war at the Alamo and the Goliad mission, at the order of their general, Santa

Anna. Knowing that the Texian rebels had blood in their eyes as a result of these war crimes, the Mexican soldados wanted to distance themselves from the atrocities as best they could. Even rank amateur Texas historians are familiar with the self-proclaimed Napoleon of the West's red flag hoisted in San Antonio, which put Alamo defenders on notice that no quarter would be given. What some of us didn't know, until informed in Kent Biffle's *Dallas Morning News* "Texana" column of March 31, 2002, was that the unmerciful Mexican general carried a license to murder in his pocket as he entered Texas to put down the Texas Revolution. Mr. Biffle points out the existence of a Mexican document known as the "Tornel Decree" after Mexican Defense Minister José María Tornel, which Santa Anna used to justify his plan to take no prisoners in the war to put down the rebellion in Texas, a plan that can only be adjudged "premeditated murder" by even the most liberal of historians.

Although the noted columnist doesn't reveal the text of the decree, he quotes Revolutionary scholar Kevin Young of San Antonio, who explained thus: "Non-Mexicans who were caught under arms fighting against the Mexican government on Mexican soil were to be treated like pirates—executed." The operative phrase in Mr. Biffle's column is "The document sought to justify Santa Anna's plan," clearly indicating the tyrant had already made the determination to punish the rebellious Texans unmercifully! We are grateful to Kent Biffle for permitting us to draw from his column the details surrounding Santa Anna's brutality. Excerpts from this column are reprinted with permission of the *Dallas Morning News*.

JUAN SEGUIN, TEJANO HERO OF THE TEXAS REVOLUTION

The only Tejano (Mexican-Texan) military unit to participate in the Battle of San Jacinto, in which Texas won her independence from Mexico, was commanded by Juan N. Seguin. Seguin was originally one of the Alamo defenders, but was sent out as a courier.

Upon reaching Gonzales, he organized a company of men that functioned as rear guard for Sam Houston's army. Seguin's was the only Tejano unit to fight in the Battle of San Jacinto. Seguin directed the burial services for the Alamo dead.

HEROIC TEXANS NOT LIMITED TO INDEPENDENCE FIGHTERS

When someone mentions heroic Texans, in our mind's eye we think of those larger-than-life figures from those days of our fight for independence from Mexico. They rode and fought "hell bent for leather" across the pages of Texas history in the 1830s, to make Texas an independent republic. Perhaps it is more than just the legends that they created that has been their legacy to their progeny? A diligent study of our contemporary history can easily convince one that their very genes have been passed on to subsequent generations of Texans. For this book we have made an effort to sift out a few examples of heroic Texans, which seems to bear out this theory.

RICHARD W. (DICK) DOWLING A Houston saloon owner who enlisted in the Confederate army and made a name for himself in Texas history, while at the same time creating a reputation of questionable notoriety for a Federal general. According to the *Handbook of Texas,* on September 5, 1863, a Federal expedition of some twenty ships carrying 5,000 troops left New Orleans, for the purpose of invading Texas. They were under the command of General William Franklin. The first objective was to capture Sabine Pass. The pass was protected by Fort Sabine, a small earthwork defended by six cannons and forty-two men, mostly Irish Houstonians under Lieutenants W. H. Smith and Richard (Dick) Dowling. Three gunboats were sent to silence the fort before landing the troops. The Confederates were so relentlessly successful against the three ships that Franklin ordered the expedition back to New Orleans and gained fame for being the first American general who managed to lose a fleet in a contest with land batteries alone.

TEXANS AND THE MEDAL OF HONOR—BRAVERY IS NO STRANGER TO TEXAS OR TEXANS The Lone Star State is a land born of revolution, and her people were forced to defend their land against foreign invasion and depredation by its Native American inhabitants. Texans have long honored their military leaders and common soldiers. The Congressional Medal of Honor was initiated in 1862 to recognize the courage and valor of the men in the Union Army in the Civil War. Most Texans, as do others, associate the Medal of Honor with wars of modern times. It should, however, be noted that this recognition for conspicuous bravery predates the memories of most of us. According to the 1992–93 *Texas Almanac*, the first Texan to receive the Medal of Honor was Sergeant John Ward of the 24th Infantry U.S. Indian Scouts. While on patrol on the Pecos River on April 25, 1875, Sergeant Ward and three companions charged twenty-five hostiles. He received the medal a month later.

One piece of trivia that is unique for the Medal of Honor occurred in Texas. The only battle in history where every military participant received the Medal of Honor took place in Texas in 1874. According to the *Handbook of Texas*, it happened in the "Buffalo Wallow Fight" in the Panhandle county of Hemphill near the Washita River. William (Billy) Dixon, carrying dispatches to Fort Supply, was surrounded by a band of Comanches and Kiowa warriors. With five companions Dixon decided to make a stand. Four of the men were wounded before noon. Dixon located a buffalo wallow about ten feet wide some distance away and ran for it, receiving a flesh wound in the leg. Dixon shouted for his comrades to come, and then ran back to carry a man who had a broken leg. All day the Indians circled the men, making occasional forays. At nightfall the Indians stopped. One man was sent to bring help but failed to find the trail. Dixon found the trail and found a body of mounted men in the distance, and discovered they were United States troops. The commander of the troops refused them ammunition, and left them promising to notify the commander of a camp in Gray County of their condition. One man was buried at Buffalo Wallow and the five survivors were taken to Fort Supply. The five survivors received the Medal of Honor on General Miles's recommendation. Yes, Texas is people and the above are just a few of the exceptional people who are a part of the tapestry that we proudly call Texas!

HAVE YOU EVER WONDERED WHO SAID IT?

Quotations are a lot like people. There are those you can never forget, and those which you can't forget quick enough! This is especially true about quotations by Texans and about Texas. We have endeavored to assemble some of the best-known of both classes, and let the reader place them in their proper category. At least you will know whom to praise, or whom to despise, depending upon your allegiance to the topic of the quotation. You, like I was, might be surprised who said what about whom!

1. Without doubt, the most unforgettable quotation in Texas history is credited to Lieutenant Colonel Sidney Sherman, for whom the North Texas city of Sherman is named. Colonel Sherman was a businessman who sold his plant and used the money to outfit a company of volunteers to fight in the Texas Revolution. Sherman is credited with coining the battle cry "REMEMBER THE ALAMO!"

2. On the reverse side of the quotation coin is a quotation that is probably the most arrogant insult to Texas ever uttered by a public servant. It, too, ironically, was made by a military man, one who, obviously, was not as enamored of the Lone Star State as many others who have championed our heritage and enjoyed our hospitality! General Philip Sheridan of Civil War fame was, according to the *Handbook of Texas*, one of the top three northern heroes of the Civil War, which may explain, but not excuse, his arrogance toward Texas. After the war President Grant ordered Sheridan to Texas with 50,000 soldiers. Reconstruction became Sheridan's primary task in Texas when he assumed command of the Fifth Military District. Sheridan became embroiled in numerous political disputes while in Texas and President Johnson transferred him from the Fifth District. Sheridan is credited with a quotation which reflected not only his disdain for Texas, but a lack of respect for her people. Sheridan was

quoted as saying, "If I owned Texas and hell, I'd live in hell, and rent Texas out!"

3. We must admit that Texans can be pretty ornery, too! And one of the state's orneriest was a man who, it has been said, was as adept at whiskey drinking and playing poker as he was at politics. John Nance "Cactus Jack" Garner, elder statesman and sage of Uvalde, Texas, the 1930s vice president under Franklin D. Roosevelt, was, based on his often-quoted, unsophisticated evaluation of his office, apparently unimpressed with it. Garner is quoted as saying, "The vice presidency ain't worth a bucket a warm spit!"

JAMES AND JOHN BEEMAN, WITNESSES TO DALLAS'S BIRTH

James Beeman was born December 21, 1816 in Illinois. In September of 1840 Beeman left Illinois for Texas. He, along with his nephew, John Beeman, crossed the line from the U.S. into Texas on December 6, 1840. He settled initially in Bowie County. Indian raids on settlers in North Texas counties made it necessary for General Tarrant to organize a troop of volunteers to deal with Indian depredations. He led the troops to Village Creek, now in Arlington, Texas, where the Keechi Indians made settling what is now Dallas and Tarrant Counties impossible. James Beeman was one of the volunteers who fought in the Battle of Village Creek, making settlement possible for whites. Following the Battle of Village Creek, John Bird got orders from General Tarrant to take troops to the vicinity of Village Creek and establish a fort. The fort became known as Bird's Fort, and John and Jim Beeman moved their families to Bird's Fort.

Colonel John Neely Bryan came to Bird's Fort and discussed his efforts to found a town where the West Fork and Elm Fork of the Trinity River came together. He planned to call his new town Dallas. Bryan was anxious for the residents of Bird's Fort to move to Dallas. John Beeman and others went with Bryan to inspect the new town site. John and Jim Beeman were favorably impressed and decided to move to Dallas. The Beemans' landing in Dallas proved fortuitous, as by this time those living in Bird's Fort had been informed that a land grant, which took in Bird's Fort, had been awarded to the W. S. Peters Company, known as the Peters Colony, and they would have to move. The families of Jim and John Beeman lived in a blockhouse that had been built in Dallas. John Neely Bryan married John Beeman's daughter, Margaret Beeman. The Beemans built homes in the White Rock Creek area, where buffaloes were often plentiful, as were Indians from time to time. They witnessed the arrival of Dallas's first settlers. They saw the development of the communities of Cedar Springs and Farmers Branch. Among the settlers at Cedar Springs was John Huitt, who became the county's first sheriff.

SOPHIA PORTER, A FRONTIER WOMAN OF MANY FACES!

In our first book, *A Treasury of Texas Trivia*, we wrote of traveling up Dallas's Preston Road to the small community of Pottsboro, near which one can visit the tiny Preston Bend Cemetery, where Sophia Porter and her husband, frontier trader Holland Coffee, are buried. We thought we had covered Sophia Porter's story pretty completely. But that was before we read the *History of Grayson County, Texas,* Vol. II, published by the Grayson County Frontier Village, Inc. in 1981. This informative volume reveals a Sophia Porter of multiple faces. The biography reads as follows: "Many colorful characters still live in county legends but none capture the imagination of Grayson County residents as completely as Sophia Suttenfield Auginbaugh Coffee Butts Porter. 'Aunt Sophie,' as she became known in later life, has been described by history writers as a heroine and devoutly religious woman, and as a prostitute and nymphomaniac. Whatever her morals she has earned a place in county history that cannot be deposed. Sophia Suttenfield was supposedly abandoned in Texas in 1836 by her husband, German army officer, Jesse Auginbaugh. She followed the Texas army during the revolution and it was probably at this time she gained a name of ill repute. She later told of nursing Sam Houston after he was wounded at San Jacinto. She married

Holland Coffee and moved to his trading post at Preston, which was sometimes called Fort Holland. Holland built Glen Eden, a showplace home for his new wife, in 1845. And the couple set out entertaining the many prominent guests who traveled through the area on the Preston Road, which connected with the Shawnee Trail or Texas Road, as it was sometimes called. Coffee was killed in an 1846 duel, which was suspected by some as being staged by Sophia. In 1846 she married George N. Butts. Butts was ambushed in 1863 and Sophia was once again a widow. In 1865 Sophia married her fourth and last husband, Judge James Porter and the couple returned to Glen Eden where she set about planting cotton with the help of her slaves, who remained of their own accord after they were freed. It was during her marriage to Porter that the noted pioneer woman 'got religion' at a camp meeting and took on a new respectability. She was always popular at Old Settler's meetings where she regaled the guests with stories from her life on the frontier. Sophia died Aug. 27, 1897 and since that time the tiniest scrap of information about the woman is told and retold. And her legend grows."

A KALEIDOSCOPE OF CULTURE

When writing about the people of Texas, some of the figures loom so large that we sometimes forget that Texas is made up not only of the individuals who have been drawn to our memories because of their fame or infamy, or those who have achieved notoriety of one sort or another. Texas is also made up of groups of people. Ever since Moses Austin and his son, Stephen, gained Empresario status and began to recruit Anglo colonists for the Texas frontier, offering the availability of vast lands, often at seemingly giveaway prices, men have been attracted to Tejas like iron filings are attracted to a magnet. Men came from all walks of life, and from all corners of the world. Not only did they come as individuals, and individual families, but they came to Texas in groups. There were Swedes, Norwegians, Czechs—and don't forget the Germans. And they brought with them more than just their household effects and a dream for a better tomorrow when they arrived from foreign shores. Each group brought its proud heritage with it, and has done a yeoman's job of preserving its ethnic culture, while at the same time sharing it with those of us who were not born into it. They have, at the same time, successfully assimilated themselves into the Texas mainstream.

All one has to do is pay a visit to the rolling, wildflower-carpeted hills of the Texas Hill Country and instantly be transported, it would appear, across the "Big Pond" to a small German dorf, where most of the signs are painted in a Gothic style that even looks guttural, and where a smattering of German is heard on the streets and in the restaurants, which, as could be expected, offer menus that feature Old World German cuisine. These residents maintain their German heritage, brought to this beautiful section of the Lone Star State in 1846 when John Meusebach came from New Braunfels and founded Fredricksburg after successfully making peace with the Comanches. Mausebach and other colonists left the old country to come to Texas in hopes of building a life of independence and personal freedom not enjoyed at the time in their native Germany. This group of new Texans put down deep and loyal roots in the wide open spaces of Texas.

We witnessed a perfect example one group preserving its ethnic heritage while at the same time sharing it with those of us outside its culture. On May 5, 2002, the 56th Saengertag (Singer's day), under the auspices of the Deutsch-Texanischer Saengerbund (German-Texan Singer League), was held in Dallas. This organization is made up of men's choirs, women's choirs, and children's choirs, largely from Texas's German communities, and whose songs are sung entirely in the German language. This highly organized endeavor makes it possible to keep alive the tradition of each dorf and town in Germany having choirs, which often competed with other singing groups.

This year's Saengertag was hosted by Dallas's own 125-year-old Frohsinn Singing Society. The determination of this group of Texas Germans to preserve their heritage can be seen in the founding dates of the participating singing groups as follows: San Antonio Liederkranz, founded 1892; Beethoven Ladies' Choir, San Antonio, founded 1932; San Antonio Men's choir, founded 1867; Frohsinn Men's Choir, Dallas, founded 1877. These German

Texans represent just one of the many ethnic groups that are a part of the kaleidoscope of culture that make up the people of Texas.

FEUDIN', FUSSIN', AND FIGHTIN': TEXAS'S FAMILY FIGHTS

As diverse as the cultures were in this vast land called Texas, it is not difficult to imagine differences of opinions arising, even among the residents of a state whose state motto is "Friendship." Perhaps it would be best if some of these "family squabbles" were left as skeletons to rattle around in the state's closet, but, in the interest of truth, and in keeping with the spirit of today's Freedom of Information laws, we feel the need to review some of the family squabbles that involved various factions in Texas.

COUNTY-SEAT WAR OF VAN ZANDT COUNTY Once again referring to the *Handbook of Texas*, Canton, county seat of Van Zandt County, Texas, was established in 1850. When the Texas and Pacific Railroad was built across the country in 1872, it missed Canton by ten miles. The citizens of Wills Point persuaded county officials to move the county seat there. In the resulting dispute, residents of Canton in 1877 went armed to Wills Point to get the county records back, and the county judge wired Governor William B. Hubbard for aid. This writer had the distinct pleasure of interviewing one-hundred-year-old Effie Thomas, who was born in Wills Point. She related how she remembered her father telling how Wills Point citizens, in anticipation of a battle, armed themselves and barricaded themselves on the roof of the Harris Hotel. The Supreme Court of Texas decided in favor of Canton. Unwilling to use the railroad at Wills Point, Canton businessmen established Edgewood ten miles northwest of town and built an extension to the railroad at a siding formerly called Stevenson.

JOHNNY RINGO AND THE "MASON COUNTY WAR" The Mason County War, commonly called the "HooDoo War," was, in the strictest sense, not a war, but a feud growing out of the stealing and killing of cattle. Many citizens of Mason County were German, or of German extraction; and neither they, nor other citizens, were able to get protection from cattle thieves. The trouble began seriously when Sheriff John Clark arrested nine men on charges of stealing cattle. Before a trial was held four of the men escaped from jail. A mob of about forty men took the remaining five from jail in February of 1875, led them to a place near Hick's Springs, and hanged them. A group of Texas Rangers followed but did not arrive in time to save them. As a result of subsequent violence, a feud developed. Scott Cooley, a former Ranger, swore revenge for the death of one of his friends, Tom Williamson. He developed a following of his own, which resulted in the deaths of at least a dozen men. One of the victims, John Worely, was shot through the head and his scalp taken. Governor Richard Cole sent a company of Texas Rangers to quiet the difficulties. It was not until after 1876 that the county settled down to respectable peace and order.

Some historians have recorded that the infamous gunslinger Johnny Ringo (who later showed up to make a name for himself slinging lead against Wyatt Earp and his brothers in Tombstone, Arizona Territory) was involved in the "Mason County War" in Texas on the side of the Cooley faction. The *Tombstone Epitaph* reported that "Johnny Ringo finally paid the price usually demanded of his ilk. He was found with a bullet through his head in July, 1882, in a lonely canyon near Tombstone. The deadliest gun of his time sleeps on for all eternity in a crude grave, without epitaph or identification. At the foot of the Chericahuas."

THE WAR WITHOUT BLOODSHED, "THE ARCHIVES WAR" In this twenty-first century many of us are of the opinion that the end of the world will be brought about not by a cataclysmic firestorm, but rather by being inundated in a deluge of the paperwork our society has created. Yet our forefathers seemed to find it necessary to protect, at whatever the cost, the paperwork of their day! We find several examples of this urgency to hold on to government-generated paperwork, even at the risk of human lives. One example provided by the Texas State Historical Association is what is called "The Archives War." In March of 1842, after Mexican forces tried to reassert their claim to Texas by moving into San Antonio and demanding its surrender, President Sam Houston called an emergency session of the Texas Congress. Fearing that the Mexicans might move on Austin, Houston had the meeting moved to the city of Houston. Historians write that citizens, fearing that Houston wanted to make his namesake city the permanent capital of the Republic, formed a vigilance committee. When officers prepared to remove some of the papers, the archives were packed into boxes, and a guard was placed over them. The *Handbook of Texas* reveals that at the end of December 1842, Houston sent a company of Rangers to Austin to remove the archives to Washington-on-the-Brazos with orders not to resort to bloodshed. The Austin vigilantes were unprepared for the raid and the Rangers were successful in their mission, loading the archives into wagons and driving away, but not before being fired upon by a cannon set off by Angelina Eberly. On January 1, 1843, however, the vigilance committee seized a cannon from the arsenal and overtook the wagon at Kenny's fort on Brushy Creek. Only a few shots were fired, with the Rangers giving up the papers to avoid bloodshed.

CAPTAIN RANDOLPH MARCY, DISCOVERER OF PALO DURO CANYON

According to the *Texas Almanac*, the Lone Star State's answer to the Grand Canyon, Palo Duro Canyon in the Texas Panhandle, which was well known to the Plains Indians, was "discovered" by Captain Randolph Marcy of the U.S. Army in 1852. The spectacular canyon exposes rocks spanning 200 million years. In 1876 it became a part of the ranching empire of legendary trail driver Charles Goodnight. The park has become a favorite destination for Texas tourists, especially campers and hikers.

THE TEXAS BRIDES WHO WORE BLACK

Just north of La Grange and still very much of that part of Texas settled by German immigrants is the picturesque town of Serbin, which was established in 1855 on 400 acres of land bought on behalf of 500 Wends who immigrated in 1854 from Germany. The

Wends, or "Sorbs," were Germans with Slavic roots who made their home just south of Berlin. The Wends spoke German and their own Wendish language. They had their own customs, which they brought with them to Texas. The land purchased for them was divided into farms and town lots that were sold to individuals. Originally called Low Pin Oak Settlement, the name of the town was changed to Serbin (Wendish Land) when the town got its post office in 1860.

One of the strange customs brought to Texas by the Wends was the practice of their brides being married in black wedding dresses. The most obvious reaction, says Evelyn Kasper of the Wendish Heritage Museum in Serbin, is "Why black?" Ms. Kasper, herself a Wend, told us that some believe it was to remind the bride that "marriage has its hardships, too." But Ms. Kasper disagrees with this explanation. She believes that it is because of Wendish frugality that black wedding dresses are worn. She explained that the custom of wearing black during the exceptionally long mourning period following a death necessitated having a black dress; an additional expense for a wedding dress was disdained by the frugal Wends. Being married in a black wedding gown made the dress practical for both occasions. We have spoken with native Berliners who are familiar with the black wedding dress custom, and who have heard the same explanation that is offered by Ms. Kasper. The Wendish Heritage Museum exhibits black wedding dresses as well as vintage photographs of Wendish weddings in which the traditional black dress is worn. A visit to the museum will enlighten the visitor in this segment of this little-known European culture tucked away in South Central Texas.

SILENT STORIES ETCHED IN STONE

The history books and genealogical archives are filled with the legends and lore of Texas. But some of the state's most interesting stories are to be found in a most unlikely place. These are the silent stories etched in the grave markers of Texas's many rural cemeteries. Only family ties or a strong curiosity causes one to stop and venture into rural cemeteries. For me it was the latter,

Those Texans who have gone on before us did much to create the Texas heritage of which we proudly brag. Much of their story is left behind in the cold stones that mark their final resting places. This cemetery at Preston Bend near Lake Texoma is typical of most rural cemeteries, except for the fact that it contains the graves of two of the state's historical figures, Sophia Porter and her husband, Indian trader Holland Coffee. Photo from author's collection.

combined with a strong imagination and an adventurer's certainty that therein lay a hidden story! The back roads of Texas are sprinkled with small old cemeteries filled with the final resting places of family members of those who settled and perpetuated the communities that they once served. I say "once," because these old "marble orchards," as we used to irreverently call them, are seldom used any more. They are not used because the folks living in these rural areas of Texas have, out of necessity, moved on to larger urban areas where opportunities are offered that are unavailable in the older rural venues.

One has to take but a few steps into one of these older cemeteries to start to notice the difference between them and urban cemeteries. When these old burial grounds were established, there was no such concept as paid perpetual care. The perpetual care given earlier in less hectic times was lovingly given by family members or a volunteer cemetery committee of the church around which many of the cemeteries were planned, as was the custom of that era. Today a visit to one of these old burial plots causes us to notice at first glance the tall, elaborate stone memorials, as well as the upright flat markers, most of which have acquired a mosslike patina mixed with weather stains, earned by years of standing sentrylike, bearing the vital statistics of the loved one whose plot they mark.

I think it is the promise of finding a hidden gem among these vital statistics that causes me to veer my car to a convenient place to park for a brief exploration before proceeding on to my destination. This was especially so on a recent visit I made to see my sister, Nell, and my dear friend, Gerti, who was recently widowed. They both reside near Lake Texoma in Grayson County. I was traversing the meandering back roads of the densely wooded area that surrounds the normally unpublicized communities of Fink and Pottsboro. When one considers that this land once bordered what was once known as Indian Territory, it doesn't take much to stir the already fertile imagination into thinking about what secrets an old cemetery in this region might hold!

Two such cemeteries that caught my eyes in this haven for nature-lovers, which is rapidly being discovered and invaded by the traffic- and crime-plagued dwellers of the Dallas area, were seen in the Preston Cove development. One was fairly large compared to what appeared to be a family burial ground, as it contained less than a dozen headstones. It was barely visible as one rounds a sharp bend in the road. It was totally surrounded by native trees and dense undergrowth. Some of the stones were fairly elaborate, and tall enough to catch one's eye. Otherwise, one would not see the burial ground sitting no more than ten yards off the road in the undergrowth that framed it.

The main reason that these two antique-appearing cemeteries piqued my interest immediately was because of the name of the area in which they were located, "Preston Cove." I had previously included in my collection of Texas trivia the story of

Dallas's fashionable Preston Road, how it was laid out in 1841, following an old Indian trail, just after Fort Preston was built on the Red River in Grayson County, and how it connected the old fort to Austin by way of Dallas and Waco. I was also aware that the old town of Preston had been covered by the waters of Lake Texoma when the U.S. Army Corps of Engineers built the dam that created the lake. The town of Preston had its beginning with the establishment of Coffee's Trading House on the Red River in 1837. Preston was an important shipping point during the Texas Republic. Preston was the location of Coffee's historic two-story mansion, "Glen Eden," which too had been submerged by the waters of Lake Texoma. One with any curiosity at all can readily see the need to explore two old tree-shrouded cemeteries such as these! What links, if any, would they offer to a once productive Texas town, a military fort, or a once elaborate plantation home that was for ninety-seven years a showplace for Grayson County, even extending its hospitality to visitors to the Texas Centennial of 1936? Glen Eden was dismantled in 1942 because it sat on land condemned for the Red River dam which created Lake Texoma.

With all this grist for my curiosity mill, I could hardly wait to get a look at the names and dates of deaths on the markers standing only a few feet from my car. I wanted to determine if these two old relics of a bygone era would permit me, in their mute way, to have a brief, if only tenuous, relationship with early settlers who made for themselves a place in the pages of history—not only the history of Grayson County, but of the Republic of Texas. Also, what legends would I find silently etched in the cold stones? My curiosity-driven quest for additional facts about the area surrounding the two burial plots increased when I learned that the area around the larger burial ground was known, officially or unofficially, which I was not sure, as "Glen Eden." Armed with this additional bit of locally provided information, I set about trying to learn if the name was only a bit of historic nostalgia, or if could I be standing in the midst of what once was Holland Coffee's plantation, on which his precious Glen Eden once stood.

If these old stones could talk! How many times have most of us remarked about some inanimate object, such as walls, "If these old walls could talk, what stories they could tell." If it's important enough to take the time, and you have the curiosity to do so, you will find that the cold marble and granite stones in an old cemetery can, in their own way, talk to you and tell you some pretty interesting and thought-provoking stories. Just a few penciled notes, taken over an hour or so, provide me with the following stories from the two Grayson County cemeteries near Pottsboro.

One of the stories told by these weathered old stones was that strong family ties existed in the nineteenth-century families. This was indicated by the groups of family graves having stones with burial dates that indicate that family members have been brought back in recent years to be buried with their ancestors. The infant mortality rate was graphically pointed out by the number of graves where dates indicated that the person died before reaching age ten. Perhaps this also tells us something about the harshness of pioneer life in North Texas in the nineteenth century, and in a way more impressive than when it's told in a textbook.

Of course, another harsh aspect of the 1800s was revealed by the stones of the young and middle-aged men who served in the Civil War of the 1860s. This stark reality was faced with obvious pride, according to the stories etched in stone. One such stone was that of William T. Caddell, whose family, possibly following his wishes, had his stone engraved to reflect his service in "Co. A of the Second Alabama Cavalry of the Confederate Army." This pride of military service in one's company was obviously handed down to the next generations of North Texans, as evidenced by at least two family markers where the family felt strong enough about their loved one's service to his country to include such details as "Sgt. U.S. Air Force World War II" and "PFC US Army." These two twentieth-century veterans matched their Civil War ancestors in one respect. They were, based on the dates on their stones, plucked in their youth and sent to fight for what was deemed a necessary cause! Such inscriptions as "In my father's house are many mansions" tell us another story. This stone reflects a willingness to publicly express the family's faith in God.

"SANCTIFIED SISTERS": TEXAS'S EARLIEST WOMEN'S LIBBERS?

A full 100 years before American women began burning their bras, spouting their doctrine of sexual liberation, filibustering for equality in the workplace, and loudly proclaiming their freedom from male chauvinism, a group of women known as "Sanctificationists," or "The Sanctified Sisters," united to form one of Texas's early efforts at Communism. Led by Mrs. Martha McWhirter, a devout Methodist, a handful of women bonded together to found a commune, originally totally excluding men.

The Belton, Texas woman, Mrs. Martha McWhirter, along with a few religious zealots started the commune in the 1860s as a result of a rift with the Methodist Church over two doctrinal issues. Mrs. McWhirter's account of the original cause of the rift was an extraordinary religious experience of hers. In 1866 she lost at short intervals two children and a brother. She regarded this as a chastisement from God, and resolved that she would try to lead a better life. While she was in this state of mind, a protracted prayer meeting was held in Belton. Mrs. McWhirter worked diligently on behalf of her unconverted children, but to no avail. At the end of the week-long meeting she was walking home one evening, when, she said, a voice within asked if she did not believe that what she had seen that week to be the work of the devil. All that night she struggled and prayed against that suggestion; but, recounted Mrs. McWhirter, the next morning while she was preparing breakfast, she experienced a kind of Pentecostal baptism, through which it became clear to her that the voice from the night before was from God. From then on, she professed sanctification and taught the doctrine in a way so as to struggle strongly with the views of her successive pastors, but not to break openly with the church.

Her convictions about her sanctification were effectively set forth in a ladies' weekly prayer meeting that was held from house to house in the Bell County town for some years after her "sanctification." This eventually merged into a meeting of her followers alone. All except seven were Methodists; of the others, five were Baptists, one a Presbyterian, and one was a "Campbellite" (Church of Christ). At length the rupture with the churches came, but the issue was one concerning sectarianism, rather than sanctification.

The second issue centered, it seemed, around a Sunday School kept by Mrs. McWhirter in opposition to one kept up by the Methodist Church. Mrs. McWhirter and her followers developed and dwelt upon their peculiar views about sanctification. None of the religious denominations in town had a building until the Methodists built one and occupied it in 1870. The pastor then organized a Methodist Sunday School. Mrs. McWhirter and her followers strongly objected to this and refused to sever their ties with the one established by Mrs. McWhirter. By this time Mrs. McWhirter and her followers were more and more out of harmony with the churches. They declared themselves no longer under the control of their pastors. The weekly prayer meetings continued and the Sisters undertook to hold them in the Methodist Church. One afternoon when they assembled there, they found it locked. They made their way in through the windows and held their usual service. In 1874 a Union church was built in Belton for the use of all denominations, except the Methodists. When it was finished, the Union Sunday School, which was under Mrs. McWhirter's superintendency, was moved into it. By the withdrawal of one denomination after another, this church building was occupied at length almost exclusively by the Union Sunday School and the Sisters, and came to be looked upon as the meeting place of the "Sanctified Sisters."

The formation of the group of "Sanctificationists," as some called them, was not without its price. Serious trouble had begun to manifest itself in the form of marital problems. An extract from one divorce petition alleges, "This band teaches and enforces the doctrine that it is sinful for a wife to live with a husband who does not believe the doctrine; such a husband is a serpent in the house, and the wife should separate and depart from him." The petition continues, "The defendant withdrew herself from the plaintiff's bed and board in 1879." Some of the Sisters that were not divorced from their husbands remained under the same roof with, but in practical separation from them, claiming to act as their servants.

Some repercussions against the Sanctified Sisters took on a more serious tone as hostility against them increased. In

February of 1880, two brothers who had previously attached themselves to the "Sanctificationists" became victims of mob hostilities. They were taken from their houses at midnight by a number of men. They were whipped most severely and ordered to leave the county.

The Sisters showed their determination to live independently from men through financial independence. They became involved in several income-producing endeavors, one of which was taking in laundry, which was done at Mrs. McWhirter's house at first, and then passed from house to house among the Sisters until one Sister's husband, who objected to the washing being done at his house, drove them away with sticks and stones. The money earned through the efforts of the Sisters was put into a common fund with Mrs. McWhirter as Treasurer. The "Sanctificationists" also sold milk and butter, producing an income of five or six dollars a day. They also produced income from nursing sick people and acting as a nurse for children. From their laundry work they earned as much as two hundred dollars a month. In addition to these money-making projects they added selling wood. Two of the Sisters had a horse and from their common fund they purchased a wagon and harness. They then bought wood at twenty-five cents per cord as it stood in the forest. They cut and hauled it themselves and sold it at three dollars per cord. The Sisters received solicitations from residents of Belton for all types of employment, such as cooking. Their common fund grew as they began to accept employment regularly. The Sisters continued to engage in domestic services regularly until 1887, at which time it became necessary to have the help of all members in the hotel they had opened the year before.

Some peculiarities of the faith held by these women who "separated themselves from the world" are pointed out by a case involving life insurance. The husband of one of the Sanctified Sisters belonged to the Knights of Honor lodge, and in 1883 he died, leaving two thousand dollars due her as a death benefit. The officers of the Belton lodge went to her with the money and sought to persuade her to take it, but she would not. She had previously declined the offer of help from the Sisters to nurse her husband before he died, and she refused to touch a dollar of his insurance when he died. As a result, her brother petitioned that she should be tried for lunacy, which was done, and she was convicted. She was sent to the asylum, but after a time was discharged as a patient but kept at the institution as a seamstress. She saved from her wages as a seamstress ninety dollars, which, upon her return to Belton, went into the Sisters' common fund.

The Sisters had built a house for one of their members who had trouble with her husband, doing most of the labor themselves. Within a year and a half from the time the first house was built, three others were built for rent, in order to invest the surplus money on hand. The women soon had renters and boarders in several houses. The Sanctified Sisters became well known in Belton for the fine table fare and clean beds they offered in their hotel and boardinghouses, which were frequented by local Belton residents of the best class. The Sanctificationists now total thirty-two in all, and have never been more than about fifty. Still in existence, the Sisters' membership now has been expanded to include others outside their original concept. Two are married men whose faith has cut them off from their families, two are unmarried young men, three are boys, nine are widows whose husbands are dead or divorced or have disappeared, eight are unmarried girls over sixteen, and eight are girls under sixteen. Two or three of the little girls have been committed to the Sisters to be reared. We are indebted to the Belton Public Library for providing us portions of George P. Garrison's "A Women's Community in Texas," which tells the story of the "Sanctified Sisters."

SAM HOUSTON'S WIFE, MARGARET, PROHIBITED BY LAW FROM BEING BURIED NEXT TO SAM

Sam Houston died July 26, 1863 in the so-called Steamboat House, in Huntsville, Texas. He is buried in Oakwood Cemetery in Huntsville. Houston's wife, Margaret Lea, died December 3, 1867 in Independence, Texas. She is buried next to her mother, Nancy Lea, in that city. Margaret Houston's biography in the *Handbook of*

Texas reveals the reason Margaret was prohibited from being buried next to her famous husband.

"In the fall of 1867, while preparing to move with her smallest children to Georgetown, she contracted yellow fever and died December 3rd at Independence, where, because of health laws, she was buried next to the tomb her mother had built for them both." Health laws required that those persons dying of the dread disease be buried the same day.

"MINNOWS IN MILK" STORY ADDS TO JUDGE ROY BEAN'S COLORFUL LORE

As if the Texas judge known as "The Law West of the Pecos" was not already saturated with enough peculiarities to choke a Mexican jackass, an incident that occurred during Judge Roy Bean's brief career in San Antonio, Texas came to our attention courtesy of my neighbor, Clarence Davenport, who has close ties with the judge's legendary Jersey Lilly Saloon in Langtry, Texas. Clarence informed me that the eccentric old codger once made his home in San Antonio and the area of Bean's business became known as "Beantown!" I immediately went to my trusty *Handbook of Texas* to search out the details surrounding Clarence's tidbit about the crusty old character. While I found one small flaw in Clarence's memory, his clue led to a Beanesque story that was worth all the detective work required to ferret it out! The story fit hand in glove with the brief reference to Bean's San Antonio venture found in the *Handbook of Texas* as follows: "Bean may have had some unofficial military experience, but he found it prudent to leave the country and begin a new life in San Antonio. In an area on South Flores Street that soon earned the name of 'Beanville.' He became locally famous for circumventing creditors, business rivals, and the law." Jana Prock, reference librarian at the San Antonio Public Library, provided a reference to an incident which not only underscores Bean's adeptness at being inventive, which served him well as Justice of the Peace, but also presents a clue as to why the old judge found it necessary to circumvent those with whom he did business. Ms. Prock sent us excerpts from Charles Ramsdell's 1976 book, *San Antonio, A Pictorial and Historical Guide,* in which the author identifies a house at 407 Glenn Avenue, about which he writes, "In the 1870s, Roy Bean, later Judge Bean, 'Law west of the Pecos' had a dairy here. When the customers found minnows in the milk, he complained his cows kept lapping them up from the river." Sounds like a case for either the Pure Food and Drug Commission or the Texas Parks and Wildlife Department!

JUSTIN RAYNAL . . . MONUMENT TO A BARKEEP

The naming of schools and erecting of monuments in Texas is generally reserved for heroes of the Texas Revolution or citizens who have been propelled into prominence by their military service or philanthropic deeds; however, Texas history shows that Texas has a way of attracting common people whose uncommon service elevates them to the ranks of those whom we honor for their heroics. Such is the case of Denison's Justin Raynal. One of the few, if not the only, Texas monuments honoring a barkeep can be seen in Denison, Texas. Controversy threatened the development of Denison's school system. The disputes were many and varied. Few, if any, of the fledgling railroad town's citizens expected the education stalemate to be nudged into positive action by a saloonkeeper. The first few years of the 1870s found Denison exploding with growth and new ideas. While the debate over the building of the town's first school was only one of the issues under consideration, it was a torrid one! Then a most unusual "knight in shining armor" rode in to serve as a catalyst for Denison's educational progress. Justin Raynal, a native of France, had opened a bar at the corner of Main and Austin, which had become a favorite venue for Denison's most influential businesspeople. The very vocal Mr. Raynal used his bar as a forum in which he urged his patrons to support building the town's first school. In addition, when the Frenchman died, he left a sizable estate to the Denison school system.

DR. LAWRENCE AUGUSTINE WASHINGTON JR.

GEORGE WASHINGTON NEVER SLEPT IN TEXAS, BUT HIS KINFOLK DID

Although George Washington never slept here, the *History of Grayson County, Texas* reminds us that the grand-nephew of America's first president, Dr. Lawrence Augustine Washington Jr., is buried in the Oakwood Cemetery in Denison, as is his wife, Martha Strewsbury Washington. According to the entry in the county's history book, George Washington's younger brother, Samuel, who died a few months after Washington's decisive victory over Cornwallis at Yorktown, left his three children, including Lawrence Augustine, under the protection of his famous brother. Although the children gave their uncle considerable trouble, George pushed them through the College of Philadelphia, and arranged for Lawrence to read law. When Lawrence died in 1824, he left his oldest son, Lawrence Augustine Jr., well fixed, but he later went broke and sold his land. In 1874 he came to Texas and settled in the year-old town of Denison. In June of 1874, the editor of the *Denison Daily News* told of visiting Dr. Washington's home and seeing a packet of letters which George Washington had written to his brother, Samuel; a sword once carried by the first president; and a suit of clothes of dark brown repp silk worn by General Washington. Dr. Washington died at Denison August 10, 1882. An official Texas Historical marker was placed at the grave of George Washington's grand-nephew in 1968.

"FATHER" R. C. BUCKNER, DALLAS'S LIVING MEMORIAL

Among the myriad of legends that fill the volumes of books written about Texas, it won't be a chore to find some folks referred to as "A legend in his, or her, own time." This flattering, and generally true, description of someone who has gained fame for his accomplishments while still alive is a fitting accolade for the man whom we choose to call a "living memorial." Many benefactors to the growth and development of a city are honored by erecting a statue or other monument to their memory, which generally details the contributions made by the individual being honored. "Father," or "Daddy" (as some of his charges preferred to call him) Buckner stood tall and straight as his own memorial or monument during his lifetime! During the 1930s and 1940s, while we grew up in Dallas, the name "Father" Buckner was as familiar to us as "Uncle Bob" Thornton became as we reached adulthood. While some legendary figures of our time were remembered for their philanthropic contribution to our city, or their political influence in getting things done, we associate "Father" Buckner's name with the type of benevolence that can't be measured in dollars and cents. For he took orphans with little hope for a future and, through the Christian nourishment of body, mind, and soul, molded their characters into useful, happy citizens of our city and state. All this was accomplished with the help of like-minded and dedicated personnel on the campus of Buckner's Orphan's Home. Although a statue of "Father Buckner," as he was lovingly called by his charges, was erected at the Home, his greatest monument is the one that can be read in the hearts and actions of the thousands of children who were products of this nurturing at the home that bears his name. Buckner's Orphan's Home in the 5200 block of south Buckner Blvd., with its numerous buildings and success-filled history, looms large as one of Dallas's major contributions to building productive citizens!

Touring this beautiful campus with its many buildings and acres of Dallas County land, one has to remember that this is a far cry from the Home's humble beginning. The *Handbook of Texas* tells us that Robert Cooke Buckner founded Buckner's Orphan's Home under the auspices of the Baptist Church. It was opened December 17, 1879 with three children occupying a cottage on a two-acre tract on Junius Street and Haskell Avenue in Dallas. Later the Home was moved to permanent quarters seven miles east of Dallas, where it was dedicated September 27, 1880. At the time of its formal opening in 1881, the Home housed eight orphans. Children of any religion are accepted at the Home and, unless adopted into private homes, are provided food, clothing, lodging, medical care, and education through high school. In 1923 the State Department of Education designated the school system of the Home as first class. After a fire in 1897, when twenty children were burned, all structures were made brick. By 1917 the plant had two thousand acres and cared for six hundred children. A hospital was built in 1932. In 1978 the Home cared for 778 orphans, 560 of which were enrolled in school. For many years the red brick buildings that make up the campus have been a familiar sight on the landscape of far East Dallas.

BUTT OF DALLASITES' RIDICULE FOUNDED BY HISTORICAL SETTLER

It is truly amazing what a little learning and a few years of maturity can do for a fellow! Although this was not very flattering to the former residents of the tiny town of Letot, which was, before it was annexed into the City of Dallas, situated along Dallas's Lombardy Lane at Harry Hines Blvd., we kids growing up in the

Nathalie and Clement Letot's grave markers are found in the Letot family plot in the Letot cemetery in Dallas. Photo from author's collection.

1930s and 1940s used this tiny town as a synonym for "Podunk." If someone had never seen or heard of something, we would ask, "Where did you come from, Letot?" The *Handbook of Texas* tells us that Letot, in northwest Dallas County near Farmer's Branch, had its post office established in 1881. The town was named for its first postmaster, Clement Letot. Other public records provide a more detailed history as follows: Clement Letot, founder of the formerly separate town of Letot, is the only veteran of the Crimean War ever known to have settled in Dallas County. A native of France who was born near Paris in 1836, he served in the French fleet that was sent to the Black Sea as part of the allied forces of Turkey, France, England, and Sardinia in their war against Russia. After the war, Letot came to the U.S. in 1860, settling in Illinois, where he farmed before moving to Texas in 1876. During the next three decades Letot became one of the wealthiest citizens of northwest Dallas County. He increased his farm and ranch holdings to 1,200 acres, engaged in various enterprises, and built his two-story farmhouse that was long a showplace in the area. An article in the April 1st, 1928 edition of Dallas's *Daily Times Herald* indicates that the eight-room frame house was built "near where Bachman's Dam is situated." During our research, we have learned, sixty-eight years later, that this is a case of inaccurate reporting. According to Kay Combel of Cavalry Hill Cemetery, who was helpful in our research of Letot, the house was built in what is now "Section D" of Cavalry Hill Cemetery on Lombardy Lane.

In the mid-1870s the Dallas and Wichita Railway was projected and built, at first as far as present Lewisville in Denton County, then to the county seat of Denton. The first of three stops on the railroad, before reaching Lewisville, was seven miles north of the Dallas County courthouse. According to the City of Dallas, maps show that this would be north of Bachman Lake at Webb Chapel and Lombardy Lane. This would have been the heart of the town of Letot. At this point land was granted by Clement Letot for a depot and the small settlement grew up which was to take the name of its leading citizen. The town was strung out along the present Lombardy Lane from Webb Chapel Road on the east to a point west of the present Harry Hines Blvd. In addition to the post office where Clement Letot was postmaster, there were also a general store, a cotton gin, and a wagon factory, all owned and operated by Letot. The town had a church, which doubled as a school on weekdays. Today the Letot school stands on the original site. It was operated by the Dallas Independent School District for years, but is now condemned and closed, after being used by the Dallas County Juvenile Department as a shelter for runaways.

One of the oldest profitable remains (pardon the choice of words) of the town of Letot is found in Cavalry Hill Cemetery on Lombardy Lane. There you will find the Letot family section. As was the custom of Texas pioneers, a plot of land on their farm or ranch was set aside as a burial ground for the family of the landowner. Such was the case of Clement and Nathalie Letot, when their son Theodore died November 27, 1884, and two months later another son, Paul, died January 28, 1885. Upon his death, on September 9, 1907, Clement Letot was buried next to his sons. Since that time there have been sixteen burials in the Letot cemetery, all Letots and kin. The last was March 5, 1980. Clement Letot was very proud of his French background, as, to my personal knowledge, are his descendants! In conversation with some of them, I was friendly, but firmly, informed that being French, the name should be pronounced "Latow," rather than the much harsher "Lee-tot" that I had, in my youthful ignorance, called it.

WHO LIES IN SAM BASS'S GRAVE?

(LEGEND AND LORE HAS NEITHER MOTHER NOR FATHER!)

Through the years of collecting and compiling our collection of Texas trivia, some items, like selecting donuts from a bakery case, were destined to become our favorites. As a former detective, I placed those posing a riddle at the top of the list. One we have especially favored was first included in the "Truth is stranger than fiction" section of our book *A Treasury of Texas Trivia,* published in 1997. That item is "Who lies in Sam Bass's grave?" This riddle is so permeated with legend and lore, we thought it should be showcased in this third volume of Texas trivia. Usually such a question as this is pretty well established, like the old joke, "Who

The Parker Memorial Cemetery in Grapevine, Texas contains the Hensley family plot where Sam Bass is believed to have been laid to rest. Photo from author's collection.

is buried in Grant's Tomb?" This trivia item, however, is not so cut-and-dried. That is precisely why it is one of our favorites.

The controversy centers around the infamous train and stagecoach robber's botched attempt, with his gang of mostly Denton County cronies, to rob the bank at Round Rock, Texas in 1887. History records that Texas Rangers were on hand to greet the Bass gang after being tipped off by one of Bass's gang members. This well-armed welcoming party was successful at giving the group a good case of lead poisoning, with Bass, according to historical accounts, succumbing from his wounds before leaving town. Legend and lore have, over the decades, spiced up our historical account of this 1887 bank robbery with many thought-provoking stories.

One such story is the basis for this item of trivia. It would have us believe that one of Bass's gang members, who was among those fatally wounded, admitted to locals that he was Bass. This was done, it is said, "to protect his leader." Bass, though seriously wounded, says the lore, managed to escape Round Rock, and was later found near Grapevine, Texas dying of blood poisoning from his wounds, and was buried in Grapevine two days later. If you talk to folks at Round Rock, as we did, you will quickly discover that they vehemently deny this lore and hold on to their story that Bass did indeed die in Round Rock with a death grip, and cite witnesses who say it took him two days to do so! They contend that he was buried in Round Rock next to a gang member.

The problem with lore such as this is finding, 118 years after the event, people to interview about the circumstances of the event. Today, even those who have heard the lore are as scarce as hen's teeth. Recently at Grapevine's Wine and Food Festival, we had the good fortune of getting a lead on this lore-based mystery from a couple of citizens, including the town's folksy but astute mayor, Bill Tate. We always imagined that if the wounded Bass did indeed manage to survive the ambush at Round Rock, he was probably attempting to reach Denton, his Texas home, when his wounds dropped him at Grapevine. We learned from Mayor Tate, who seems well versed in the Bass lore, that our theory was not altogether true! Mayor Tate told us that Bass had family living in Grapevine, which was nearer to safety than struggling to Denton. Another thing Mayor

Tate told us that piqued our interest was that when he was nine years old, he used to go with his father when he went to hoe the cemetery. He related that he distinctly remembered that while hoeing the "Old Hall" Cemetery, which is over a hundred years old, in nearby Lewisville, "I saw a grave marker which was inscribed 'Sam Bass.' " Although this marker could have been for another deceased by the same name, it interested him enough that he didn't forget it over the years. In a conversation with the caretaker at the "Old Hall" Cemetery, he recalled no such marker.

Over the years of doing our sleuthing of Texas legend and lore, the one universal truth that we have discovered is that each fragment we have uncovered about a piece of lore may be at variance with the other fragments. This is probably true because lore has neither father nor mother. Generally it is the offspring, sometimes illegitimate, of imagination or innuendo, nourished by some morsel of fact! Sometimes the fact is a product of a family story, embroidered a bit each time it has been retold. In an attempt to verify the intriguing story that the infamous Sam Bass was not, in fact, buried in his well-publicized grave in Round Rock, but instead in the Denton County town of Grapevine, we were able to find a story that bore out the alleged Grapevine burial. The most difficult element in lore-chasing is, in most cases, the passage of time. Seldom are witnesses remaining to be questioned about the facts surrounding the folklore. Occasionally, as in the case of the bank robber, alleged witnesses, in the form of descendants, have left behind written records pertaining to the incident in question. Such a record was found in the book *Grapevine Area History*, published by the Grapevine Historical Society, excerpts from which we reprint by permission, as follows: "The story of Sam Bass, a famous Texas character, is printed as written by Billie Sparger. 'Sam Bass was my great grandpa Hensley's brother-in-law. James A. Hensley married Virginia Bass.' " In writing about the Round Rock incident, Billie Sparger wrote, "'Several of the gang were killed that day. Sam, himself, was mortally wounded. The Sheriff picked up one young man yelling, "I shot Sam Bass!" They hauled the dead man through the town. Yelling all the way, "Sam Bass is dead, come see Sam Bass!" They buried the poor man in the Round Rock Cemetery. Even today people come from all over to see the grave. Sam, though badly wounded, managed to make it to the railroad tracks not far away, so I have always been told. The story goes that when the train got to Grapevine, Sam was, indeed, dead. The man at the depot knew James Hensley. He sent a man to tell him to come about Sam. According to Grandpa Hensley, when he got there, the main man at the depot had Sam dressed, wrapped him in a blanket and placed in a pine box. Grandpa paid him and told him to keep quiet about Sam. Hensley did a lot of business there so he knew he could trust him. James Hensley and two black men who lived at the ranch, Dad Nelson and another man placed Sam on a wagon and buried him by lantern light in a secret place, where he could rest in peace.' "

Another piece from the same book says that Bass's body was buried during the night at Parker Memorial Cemetery near the Hensley family plot. This is also in Grapevine. While we must depend solely on the writer's account of the death and burial of Sam Bass, both variations of the burial conflict with the historical and local accounts of this incident.

THE U.S. PRESIDENT WHO HAD NEVER SEEN HIS TEXAS BIRTHPLACE

Although thousands of Americans visit the Denison, Texas birthplace of President Dwight David Eisenhower annually, the world-famous hero of World War II, born October 14, 1890 in Denison, Texas, never saw his place of birth until June of 1945, when a delegation of Denisonians traveled to Abilene, Kansas and presented the general with a photo of his home in Denison. Eisenhower was the son of a KATY Railroad employee stationed in the North Texas city founded by the railroad. The president's official biography, according to Jack McGuire's book, *KATY Baby (The Story of Denison, Texas)*, listed Eisenhower's birthplace as Tyler, Texas. The confusion may have happened, according to author McGuire, because the Eisenhowers moved from Denison to Tyler for a time before returning to their original home in Abilene, Kansas. Acting on a tip that Ike's birthplace was actually Denison, Texas, reporters started digging into Eisenhower's background. According to records at the Tone Abstract Company, the Eisenhowers did in fact own a house in Denison in 1890. Author McGuire goes on to say, "As soon as the father accumulated enough money, they returned, via Tyler, to Abilene, the cattle town where Ike was to grow up." Later Mrs. Eisenhower was to verify that he was born in Denison, Texas.

HOWARD HUGHES, TEXAS'S BIZARRE BILLIONAIRE

Howard Hughes (1905–1976) was one of the twentieth century's best-known characters. "Sonny," as he was called by the family, grew up among the wealthy of Houston. Scion of the owner of the very successful Hughes Tool Company, there was practically nothing, or nobody, he thought he could not buy! According to the *Handbook of Texas*, Hughes grew up very close to his mother, who constantly worried about her son's health. At the slightest hint of an epidemic, she would take him out of town. In 1919 Hughes was paralyzed for a short time by an unexplained illness; the young man developed a phobic regard for his health.

While home from private school in Boston one time he took a plane ride with his father. This stimulated a lifelong love for aviation. Upon the sudden death of his father, Howard Hughes gained access to the family estate. After a quarrel with his family, Howard Hughes bought out his relatives' interest in the company.

In 1925 he married Houston socialite Ella Rice. Howard decided he wanted to make movies; so, it was off to Hollywood for Ella and Howard. Howard opened a film studio as a subsidiary of Hughes Tool Company. Hughes filmed the epic "Hell's Angels," a film about air warfare in World War One. He wrote the script and directed the picture. It was during the filming of "Hell's Angels" that Howard Hughes took flying lessons and got his pilot's license. Perhaps Howard Hughes's most famous, or infamous, production was the 1941 film "The Outlaw," starring the full-figured Jane Russell, who was studying acting at a Hollywood acting school when her thirty-eight-inch bustline came to his attention when he was conducting a chest hunt for the starring role. This film was very controversial because of the promotional material used. Some Dallas theaters refused to exhibit the film's colored posters, which exploited Miss Russell's abundant cleavage, calling the posters offensive to public decency.

But it was in aviation that the billionaire playboy excelled. Howard Hughes set a new land speed record of 352 mph with his H1, a plane he built, and which he called a "winged bullet." In 1936 he set a new transcontinental speed record, and the next year he shortened the record to seven hours and twenty-eight minutes. Hughes next converted a Lockheed 14 for an around-the-world flight. He cut Lindbergh's record in half in his flight to Paris. Hughes personally piloted the plane on the flight. The Houston billionaire circled the globe in three days, nineteen hours and seventeen minutes. On November 16, 1942, Hughes Aircraft won a contract to build flying boats to ferry men and material across the ocean. One flying boat (the one and only one he built), the HK1 (dubbed the "Spruce Goose," because it was made of plywood), was successfully flown by Hughes on October 11, 1943. It was said by some to be the largest plane ever to fly.

After his failed marriage to actress Jean Peters, Hughes became increasingly reclusive. He practically became a hermit in his rented Desert Inn penthouse in Las Vegas. Those who saw the movie about his life will remember that his paranoia about his health, including his phobia about germs, caused him to conduct most of his business by memos rather than have personal contact with people. The movie showed how the once virile-looking dark-haired young man with the Clark Gable mustache metamorphosed into a stooped old man with long matted hair and a beard to match. In poor health and with a squadron of personal aides, he went into exile in various foreign cities. In April of 1976 Howard Hughes boarded a plane en route to a Houston hospital, but died before reaching his hometown.

HARTLEY EDWARDS: A SIGNAL HONOR FOR DENISONIAN

No doubt long ago fallen though the cracks of our historic remembrances is the historic honor that fell to Hartley Edwards of Denison, Texas. Edwards earned his place in world history at

11:00 a.m. on November 11, 1918 at Tour, France when he placed a $6.25 GI issue bugle to his lips and blew "taps" as the official signal that World War I had ended. The Texan was, as personal bugler of General of the Army John J. "Blackjack" Pershing, officially ordered by Pershing to use his bugle to notify the world that armistice had been signed at Compiègne Forest in France. The Texan was at first reluctant to blow "taps" at 11:00 a.m., as taps is generally reserved for "lights out." He quickly rethought his reluctance when told that his orders came directly from General Pershing; thus he earned a footnote in the pages of world history.

U.S. ARMY FLYER LT. MOSS LOVE

In September 1913, U.S. Army flyer Lt. Moss Love was killed in a training flight in San Diego, California. In 1914 a WW I flying field was built in Dallas. The field was named in honor of Lt. Love. The city of Dallas later bought the field and it became the city's commercial airport, Love Field.

LT. BENJAMIN FULOIS: "MIDWIFE" AT BIRTH OF U.S. ARMY AIR CORPS

The United States Air Force was born right here in Texas in February of 1910 when Lt. Benjamin Fulois arrived at Fort Sam Houston in San Antonio, Texas with seventeen crates containing an airplane, accompanied by a number of student mechanics. Fulois, assigned to the aviation section of the U.S. Army Signal Corps, had taken three flying lessons from Wilbur Wright. Because of the winter weather at the Signal Corps facility at College Park, Maryland, flight training was shifted to Fort Sam Houston. Along with the seventeen crates, Fulois had orders to put the plane together, learn to fly it, and train others to fly it. The aircraft was a Wright Brothers biplane, with a wingspan of thirty-six feet and four inches, and an overall length of thirty-two feet and ten inches. The power plant was a four-cylinder, water-cooled 30.6 horsepower Wright engine. Instead of wheels, the plane was equipped with sleighlike runners. Takeoff was aided by a sort of catapult. The plane was ready to fly by March. By the U.S.'s entrance into World War I in 1917, the U.S. Army Signal Corps had thirty-five trained pilots and 200 planes. Fulois proved that airplanes could be a vital part of military operations, and helped establish Texas as a major military aviation center.

SADIE BARRETT: AN EARLY TEXAS ARMY BRAT'S RECOLLECTIONS OF HISTORIC OLD FORT RICHARDSON

Nearly three quarters of a century has passed since Sadie Barrett's father, Bill Riggs, was Stable Sergeant for the 131st Field Artillery stationed at Jacksboro's Fort Richardson. The 131st Field Artillery was part of the 36th Infantry Division of the Texas National Guard, which gained fame during World War II as "The Lost Battalion." These Texas troops were captured by the Japanese and were forced to help build the famous "Bridge over the River Kwai." The historic old Indian fort served as a National Guard Armory from 1922 until 1954.

Sergeant Bill Riggs's family was farming in the Jacksboro area when he reported one day each week for National Guard duty at nearby Fort Richardson to drill in marching and shooting, recalls Mrs. Barrett. "My Daddy was in charge of the army's horses and stables before the army was motorized," she added. "These stables," said Marjorie Sewell, historian-interpreter at the Fort Richardson State Park, "were not part of the original old fort, but were built after the fort was decommissioned." "I was a young girl in my teens at the time," said Sadie. "Some military children were known as 'Army Brats' even in those days. The year was 1928. My father made us toe the line. He didn't want us to be called Army brats." Some of the fort's early buildings still stood and were in use when Mrs. Barrett and her siblings played on the drill field. "We were not 'brats' in the dictionary sense of the word. Sgt. Riggs saw to that! We were mischievous, but not unruly. When the boys were marching, we would wait until

Daddy had stepped into the fort and then we would join the soldiers in their ranks. They would hide us so daddy couldn't see us. The army moved a big house onto the grounds not far from the old stone fort. That is where our big family lived. I remember how neat the grass was always mowed. I remember what fine, big horses the army had for pulling their huge wagons. We kids used to ride them bareback. In the barn, each horse had its own stall with its name on it. The horses were trained to go into their own stalls to be fed."

I felt fortunate to have gained this first-person remembrance of soldiering in the latter days of historic Fort Richardson. During America's westward expansion during the nineteenth century, when settlers faced the hostilities of the Native Americans whose hunting lands were being taken away from them foot by precious foot, wagon trains were at peril as they crossed the plains of Texas, as were homesteaders. This required the U.S. government to establish a network of army forts along the vast Texas frontier. One such fortification was Fort Richardson, which, the *Handbook of Texas* tells us, was established in February of 1868 to provide protection against marauding bands of Comanche and Kiowa Indians on the North Texas frontier. It was named for Union general Israel Bush Richardson. Located one-half mile south of Jacksboro, in Jack County, the fort was the northernmost army outpost in Texas. From 1868 to 1873, it was considered, strategically, the most important army post in Texas. In 1872 it had the largest garrison (666 officers and men) among military installations in the United States.

Fort Richardson was home to some of the best-known army units, which distinguished themselves in making Texas safe for settling. It was regimental headquarters for the Sixth U.S. Cavalry and the Fourth U.S. Cavalry. Fort Richardson was also home to the Eleventh Infantry, as well as various elements of the famed Tenth U.S. Cavalry, known as the "Buffalo Soldiers." The troops at Fort Richardson also helped local officers keep the peace and pursue criminals and deserters. Escorting wagon trains was a regular assignment. The army abandoned the post in May of 1878. In 1963 the fort was declared a National Historic Landmark.

Sadie Barrett's family's twentieth-century relationship with that historic old fort makes her story worth preserving, because Stable Sergeant Bill Riggs's service at Fort Richardson was, in its own way, just as vital to the strengthening of our country's defenses against our enemies as were the exploits of the "blue coats" of the U.S. Army who rode against the Comanche and Kiowa warriors from the gates of old Fort Richardson in the 1800s! Sadie Barrett didn't live to see her father's story in print. She died peacefully at age eighty-six on Sunday night, August 11, 2002.

DID YOU EVER WONDER WHAT HAPPENED TO DOCTOR JOHN BRINKLEY, THE GOAT GLAND CHARLATAN?

We are indebted to the *Handbook of Texas*, published by the Texas State Historical Association, for this insight into one of Texas's most controversial figures. "Doc" John R. Brinkley (1885–1942), who promised the sexual rejuvenation of men through the implantation of goat glands, was born in North Carolina. He was educated in a one-room school in Tuckaseigee, North Carolina, but never earned a diploma. He attended several diploma mills, such as Bennett Medical College in Chicago and Eclectic Medical University of Kansas City. Despite dubious credentials, he was licensed by the state of Arkansas and set up a medical practice in Milford, Kansas. In 1918 he began performing his controversial "goat gland operations," designed to restore male virility and fertility by implantation of goat glands. Before long more than 100 customers a week were receiving the $750 rejuvenation operations.

As a result of the rejuvenation operations and a large patent medicine business, "Doc" Brinkley became extremely wealthy. In 1923 he constructed the first radio station in Kansas, KFKB, a powerful station that carried country music and fundamentalist preaching. The American Medical Association attacked "Doc" Brinkley for diagnosing illnesses and prescribing medicines over the radio. Consequently, in 1930 the Kansas Medical Board revoked Brinkley's medical license, and the Federal Radio Commission refused to renew his radio license. Brinkley responded by entering the race for governor, hoping to appoint new members to the Medical Board. He lost his bid for election in a close race, and subsequently lost in other attempts at election.

In 1931 Brinkley received authority from Mexican officials to build a powerful transmitter in Villa Acuña, Mexico, across the river from Del Rio, Texas. In 1933 he moved his entire medical staff and facilities to the Roswell Hotel in Del Rio. He used his station, XER, to entice listeners to visit his clinic or buy an array of gimmicks. In Texas he rarely implanted goat glands, but substituted what he described as "commercial glandular preparations." Estimates are that he earned $12 million between 1933 and 1938. He battled the Internal Revenue Service over back taxes and in 1941 he was forced to file for bankruptcy. The following year circulation problems led to the amputation of one of his legs. On May 26, 1942, John Brinkley died of heart failure in San Antonio, Texas. He is buried in Memphis, Tennessee.

LOUIS WRIGHT, SHERMAN'S FIRST NEGRO JUROR

The *History of Grayson County, Texas* recorded the family history of Louis Wright, who was the first Negro to sit on a jury in Sherman. Mr. Wright was born in 1895 in a log house with a chimney constructed of mud and sticks near Lake Dallas, which was then known as Lummel Lake. After working in all manner of laboring jobs, he moved to Sherman in 1913, where in 1928 at age thirty-three he was selected to sit on the jury of a murder trial. This was the first time a Negro had been allowed to sit on a jury in that North Texas city. This experience might have prompted him to say, "Texas is the most outstanding state in the union. Its people friendly. The American people are beginning to think of all people and races. And once you get a man to think, you can work with him." It surely took more than "walking behind a team of mules in a cotton field," as he remembered doing, for a man with a second-grade education to think like Louis Wright did!

THE PEOPLE OF ATHENS AND THE BANK THAT REFUSED TO CRASH!

October 29, 1929 will always be remembered as "Black Tuesday" in America. It was on this day that the crash of the stock market set thousands of Americans on a path of self-destruction, leaping from the windows of office buildings, unable to bear the loss of a lifetime of accumulated wealth. But the plummeting stock prices would send many times that number running pell-mell to their banks and other financial institutions to draw out their cash. This "run on the banks," as it was called, in 1933 resulted in President Roosevelt declaring a cooling-off period and closing all banks temporarily. The banks reopened as soon as the bank holiday was over. Many banks, whose assets were not sufficient to meet the demands of its depositors, closed their doors for good. "The run on the banks" resulted in many bank failures

The centennial celebration of Athens First National Bank in 1990 was a spirited one, with bank employees dressing in costumes that were in fashion when the bank opened in 1890, while conducting twentieth-century business. Photo courtesy of Matt Mattison.

and a total loss of confidence in banks in the minds of millions of Americans.

Although not a Texas legend per se our neighbor, Malcolm "Matt" Mattison, brought us a little bit of Texas banking history that we feel reflects the spirit of Texas, and the people of Texas, in a way that warrants its being captured in print! It is the story of one Texas bank whose spunk and assets made it "The bank that refused to crash"! The story you are about to read is the story of the First National Bank of Athens, Texas, where Matt worked as a loan officer prior to his retirement. In addition to that city's fame as the black-eyed pea capital of Texas, this Henderson County city is the home of one of the few banks in Texas whose doors were not slammed shut as a result of the Crash of 1929. The bank was founded by Clint Murchison Sr., the father of Dallas businessman and original owner of the Dallas Cowboys football team, Clint Murchison Jr. The bank celebrated its centennial year in 1990.

In a conversation with the bank's president, Rusty Workman, we were told that the First National Bank of Athens "had been in continuous operation since its 1890 founding, and had never closed for any reason, except for the bank holiday required by President Roosevelt. The bank reopened as soon as the holiday was over." Former bank president Lavelle Layfield advised us that "There was another bank in Athens that closed (failed) during that time, but not First National." When asked how the bank had managed to remain open in spite of the country's financial panic, Mr. Workman replied that the bank was financially sound and had ample assets. "We had no reason to close!" explained the president confidently! But banks are not just money! Banks are people, too! And the folks of Athens had faith and confidence in the folks at First National in Athens. Matt told how there were several families among Athens's uncommon "common folks" who, because of sickness, poor crops, or just unexpected expenses, came to First National to borrow two or three hundred dollars each year. They were never turned down and always paid off their loans. It was this kind of "folksy" banking that commanded confidence and appreciation by the people of Athens.

The bank's centennial celebration, pointed out Matt Mattison, was a festive occasion for both customers and employees. All employees dressed in period costumes and employees and customers alike oohed and ahhed over the bronze plaque bearing the names of the bank officers in 1890 and in 1990 that was unveiled as a high point of the festive celebration. Yes, the bank had to have the assets to keep from failing during the early 1930s, but it was also the confidence of these Athens depositors, and the character of the bank's employees, that made this small Texas town's bank "The bank that refused to crash"!

INTRODUCING A FEW TEXAS FOLKS WHO LED MORE-THAN-COMMON LIVES!

THE "OOOMPH-GIRL" FROM TEXAS, ANN SHERIDAN This film star was born February 21, 1915 in Denton. She was christened Clara Lou Sheridan. For a brief time she attended North Texas State Teacher's College, which is now University of North Texas. In 1933 she was one of thirty-three young women chosen to promote a Paramount film by taking part in a beauty contest. She won a contract. Her first five films were Westerns. Publicity releases soon billed her as "The Ooomph-Girl" of the movies. She was under contract to Warner Brothers and soon reached stardom.

BOWIE COUNTY'S LARGEST BABY WENT ON TO FAME AND FORTUNE This physical description might not be much of a surprise to those of us who watched him so many years on TV, although we might not have known he was a native son of Texas. He was born in De Kalb, Bowie County, Texas in 1928. He was reported to be the largest baby born in Bowie County, weighing in at fourteen pounds at birth. He was over six feet tall and weighed 200 pounds at age twelve. By the time he was a star football player at Sul Ross University at Alpine, Texas, he was six feet four inches and weighed 275 pounds. This real Texas-size Texan was born Bobby Don Blocker, and went on to star as Dan Blocker, playing "Hoss" Cartwright on the popular TV show *Bonanza!*

FRANK HAMER BROUGHT AN END TO BONNIE AND CLYDE Francis Augustus Hamer, known as Frank or "Pancho," enlisted in the Texas Rangers in 1906. Captain Hamer resigned from the Rangers several times, only to return to fight crime in Texas. In 1932 he was recalled to duty by Governor Miriam A. (Ma) Ferguson to track down the infamous bandit team of Clyde Barrow and his poem-writing girlfriend, Bonnie Parker, who made themselves a national legend and folk heroes to many, who thought them champions of the poor in the Depression Era. After a three months' search, Hamer, with the assistance of other lawmen, trapped the pair whose names struck terror in the hearts of bankers and lawmen alike near Gibsland, Louisiana. They were shot to death in a Hamer-engineered ambush. This wrote finis to the notorious Bonnie and Clyde.

D. R. (DEE) HARKEY, THE EX-RANGER AND YOUTHFUL INDIAN FIGHTER This distant cousin of the author used his Texas law enforcement experience and bravery to help bring law and order to New Mexico. Although you might not find D. R. (Dee) Harkey in the Texas history books per se, he personifies the Devil-may-care spirit that became necessary for survival in early Texas. "Dee" Harkey was born March 17, 1866 at Richland Springs, San Saba County, Texas. While growing up on a Texas farm, it fell his lot to be raised by an older brother, Joe, after their father died. During these times of 1869 and 1870, the Comanche Indians depredated in that country. In his autobiography, *Mean as Hell*, he wrote how "they killed many people and stole everything they could get their hands on!" The people of that community organized a Ranger company, called a "minute company." His brother, Joe (although very young), was a member of the company and made a lieutenant. By 1873 the Texas Legislature passed a law making Rangers peace officers. In 1880 Joe was elected Sheriff of San Saba County. "Dee" went to work as deputy at age sixteen; he stayed there four years until he was twenty.

In 1890 Harkey moved to Eddy, New Mexico, which is now Carlsbad. As New Mexico history will show, "Dee" Harkey was made a deputy U.S. Marshall and served as cattle inspector for the

Cattle Raisers Association. Neither position made him many friends in this lawless territory. One of "Dee" Harkey's missions was to make Carlsbad a decent, law-abiding place for settlers. Although his book *Mean as Hell* points out that "Harkey never killed anyone without giving them a chance to surrender," he tells many stories of assassination attempts on his life by those whose outside-the-law endeavors he had interfered with, to put it mildly. With this in mind, it seems highly probable that Harkey might have failed to recall those instances which involved the maxim "Shoot first, and ask for surrender later." One thing which cannot be disputed is that, hated and feared by those outside the law, "Dee" Harkey found it necessary to employ all the skills he had learned at a young age as a lawman and Indian fighter back in Texas! My cousin "Dee" Harkey said adios to public service in 1911.

ELECTRA WAGGONER BIGGS

Famed Texas sculptress and oil and ranching heiress Electra Waggoner Biggs, who built Arlington Downs Race Track in the 1930s, and who was the great-granddaughter of cattle baron Dan Waggoner, was the inspiration for naming the North Texas city near Wichita Falls, Electra. She was also the inspiration for naming an American automobile, the Buick Electra, as well as the American-built Lockheed Electra. The acclaimed sculptress sculpted the statue of Will Rogers astride his horse, "Soapsuds," that stands in front of Will Rogers Memorial Auditorium in Fort Worth. The statue is entitled "Into the Sunset." It was completed in 1939 but not unveiled until 1947.

ONE OF TEXAS'S BLOODIEST LEGENDS STILL DRAWS CROWDS!

When Clyde Chesnut Barrow stole his first car at age seventeen in Dallas County, it is doubtful he gave thought to ever becoming a Texas legend. Born in Ellis County in 1909, the son of an illiterate field hand, Clyde was just the right age to disdain his meager

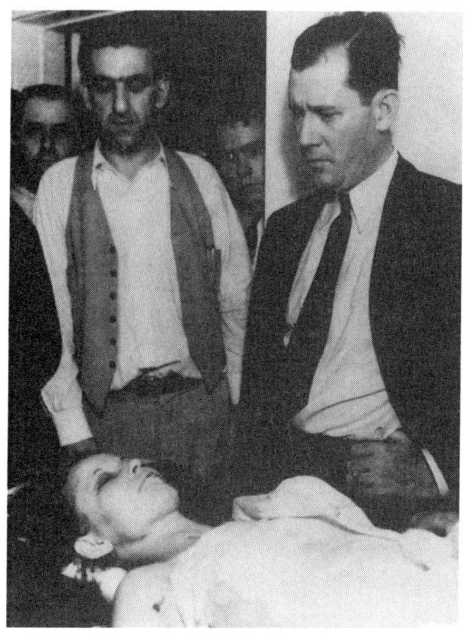

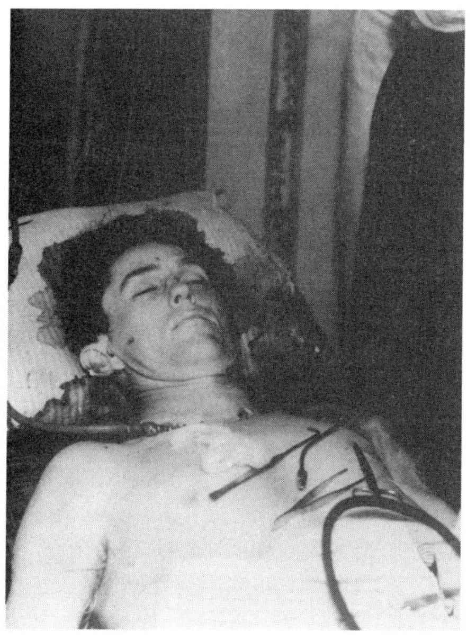

These photos of Clyde Barrow and Bonnie Parker were taken in Arcadia, Louisiana shortly after they were removed from their bullet-riddled death car. The bodies of both were sent to Dallas for their funerals. Seen gazing at the body of Bonnie Parker, the dark-haired man in the dark suit and tie is a young deputy sheriff from Dallas County by the name of "Bill" Decker. Mr. Decker went on to be one of Texas's legendary lawmen and served as Dallas County's highly respected sheriff for many years. Photos from author's collection.

existence and harbor the feelings that having a car of his own would make him "somebody"—even if it meant taking it from somebody else! Of course Clyde's reasoning for that crime that resulted in his first arrest—in 1926 in Dallas—is purely conjecture. But what isn't conjecture is the historical fact that this, one of Clyde's minor offenses, kicked off a life of crime that was to last eight terrifying years, and which would include a litany of crimes consisting of numerous armed robberies, assaults, kidnapping, and at least a dozen cold-blooded murders! Many of these crimes were committed by the nattily dressed product of Dallas's crime-infested West Dallas accompanied by the other half of the Texas legend of "Bonnie and Clyde," the diminutive (4'10", eighty-five pounds) strawberry blonde Bonnie Parker, born in Rowena, Texas, and nineteen months younger than Clyde. During their two years together during the years of the Great Depression, the pair would spray their death-dealing lead across Texas and several Midwestern states. Their bloody trail was exposed by jet-black headlines in America's most prominent newspapers. Back home in Dallas, where the seemingly conscienceless pair often sneaked to secret rendezvous with their families to enjoy Clyde's favorite foods, fried chicken and beans and cornbread, the notorious pair were heralded as modern-day Robin Hoods!

But the Texas government eventually got a bellyful of being made a fool of by this pair of illiterate punks with a penchant for murder and mayhem! Retired Texas Ranger Captain Frank Hamer was called back to duty with orders to "Take Bonnie and Clyde—Dead or Alive!" Hamer took up the hunt for the murderous pair like a bloodhound. Joined by Dallas Deputy Sheriffs Ted Hinton and Bob Alcorn, and DPS officer Manny Gault, the now public enemies were trailed to the small Louisiana farming community of Gibsland, where the pair that had terrorized several states had stopped to visit former gang member Henry Methvin.

Having been joined by Bienville Parish Undersheriff Prentice Oakly and Sheriff Henderson Jordan, the lawmen set a trap for the wanton killers. As their stolen V-8 Ford screeched to a halt at the site of the police ambush, the pair was ordered to surrender. Clyde stepped on the gas and set the car into motion. With this, the hidden officers opened fire, pumping a fusillade of bullets into the pair's fleeing automobile. A local undertaker, to whom the bodies were first taken before being shipped back to Dallas for burial, reported that each of the gangsters were riddled with dozens of the officers' bullets.

But that May day in 1934 was not the end of Bonnie and Clyde! It put an end to their reign of terror during those already painful Depression years, but it was only the beginning of the public's interest in the legend of Bonnie and Clyde! Hyped, no doubt, by the 1968 Warren Beatty–Faye Dunaway movie "Bonnie and Clyde" and further fueled by our parents' contemporary, unexaggerated tales of the rampaging pair of Texas gangsters, their infamy only whets our appetite for more information about the legendary criminals. The Dallas Historical Society told us, "Bonnie and Clyde are a hot historical item. We receive many inquires about the notorious pair." The Historical Association built an extensive Bonnie and Clyde exhibit in the Hall of State Building for the 2001 Texas State Fair. Thousands of fairgoers streamed through the exhibit and oohed and ahhed at the Bonnie and Clyde memorabilia, proving that the 1930s bandits' legend lives and draws a crowd!

GUS THOMASSON, A WASHINGTON CONNECTION

Residents of the east Dallas County city of Mesquite who daily traverse one of the city's main traffic arteries, Gus Thomasson Road, wind their way home or to neighboring shopping centers with little thought to the man for whom the road is named, nor do they realize how immersed in federal history the street is. We were reminded of the close ties this well-traveled street has with Washington, D.C. when we opened our *Dallas Morning News*' July 17th, 2002 edition. News reporter Joe Simnacher enlightened us with his vignette reviewing the forgotten namesake of this Mesquite main traffic artery, including a photo of the late Mr. Thomasson. Mr. Simnacher succinctly outlined the responsibilities of this former farm boy during the era of America's Great Depression. The reporter writes that "This one time farm boy was responsible for construction of $100 million in Depression-era projects in North Texas. One road is named for him. From 1935 until 1942, he was director of the Works Progress Administration—later named the Works Projects Administration—which helped many survive the harsh economic times of the 1930s and early 1940s." I remember how detractors had their own tongue-in-cheek name for the WPA; they said it stood for "We Piddle Around." Reporter Simnacher continues, "His projects include the Rockwall County courthouse, the Highland Park water system and Harry Hines Boulevard, as well as many parks roads and bridges." Doesn't sound much like "Piddling Around" to me! He was proud no scandal or misuse of public funds touched the WPA under his watch. When the WPA was shut down he was named district director of the Office of Price Administration (OPA), established to prevent wartime inflation. He oversaw thirty-two offices for forty Texas counties. "Reinhardt-Mesquite Road was renamed Gus Thomasson Road in 1938."

Further adding to this street's federal connection is a historical fact we wrote about in our first Texas trivia book, *A Treasury of Texas Trivia*. "A community that existed where Gus Thomasson crossed Highway 80, which was called Thin Gravy or Mesquite Tap, was, following the sudden death of President Franklin D. Roosevelt, in 1945, renamed in honor of the new president, Harry S. Truman. Truman, Texas came into being on Nov. 21, 1945 when resident, Mrs. E. H. Hopkins christened the town into existence with a bottle of milk. It is said that there being so many Baptists in the community milk was substituted for the usual champagne! Truman was eventually annexed into Mesquite." Gus Thomasson died in August of 1954. We are grateful to Joe Simnacher and the *Dallas Morning News* for permitting us to use Joe's report on Gus Thomasson.

GENERAL LUCIUS CLAY: FROM TEXOMA LAND TO BERLIN

In 1939 Captain Lucius D. Clay of the U.S. Army Corps of Engineers was assigned the job of constructing the Denison dam that created Lake Texoma. In 1948, that same Lucius Clay, this time a general, organized the famous Berlin airlift that broke the Soviet blockade of that city.

DR. RENÉ G. GERARD

Although his name is hardly known outside his hometown of Denison, Texas, Dr. Gerard has touched the lives of millions of Americans. Dr. Gerard conceived the idea of a nationwide telephone number for reporting emergencies. Through his efforts the concept was enacted by the U.S. Congress and a nationwide emergency number (911) became a vital part of America's life.

ROBERT E. SPARKMAN: A LEGACY OF HOAXES AND GOOD DEEDS

Maybe you can remember, as I do, as a small boy in the late 1930s and early 1940s, a newspaper story with the dateline Italy, Texas, telling of "Texas' own Lochness Monster"? Attention was instantly drawn to this sleepy Ellis County town by the terrifying account of the sighting of a serpentlike monster billed by the writer as "Texas' own Lochness Monster." According to the *Dallas Morning News* article, the creature had been seen near the Mill Creek bottoms. I recall that my mother was, as would be most mothers, appalled to read that the disappearance of some small children of migratory workers was credited to this serpent. Some descriptions offered by those saying they had seen the "monster" were greatly exaggerated! One man's description had the snake crossing the road in front of his automobile. The driver said, "Its eyes shone as bright as car lights." The monster was blamed every time a farmer's fence was torn down, or a cow was drowned in the Trinity River.

The monster was first reported by Robert E. Sparkman, a "stringer" (rural reporter) for the *Dallas Morning News*, who lived in the sleepy town of Italy. Mr. Sparkman filed the snake story after a wagon of a circus train traveling from Italy to Waco overturned, releasing some animals, including some snakes. Local residents having farms in the creek bottoms began sighting some of the exceptionally large (for that area) snakes. Their sightings became greatly exaggerated. These stories were perfect grist for the mill, or typewriter, of Mr. Sparkman, who had been a stringer for the *News* for twenty years, and who had developed a penchant for submitting tall tales to the *News* and the various wire services. The wire services carried the tales across the nation and around the world. Mr. Sparkman embellished the snake hoax to the point that he had the snake fifty feet long and had eyes as big as a locomotive light.

Sparkman continued to write to supply the demands of the news media. Although gasoline, due to World War II, was rationed, people were flocking to the Ellis County town to try to get a look at the monster, saving their rationing stamps to do so. Even though the reporter threw in a story about an invisible wall that the government had built to protect a secret military project from prying eyes, people continued to believe in the hoax. As Sparkman's absurdities grew, readers begged for more. Sparkman finally wrote that the serpent had crawled behind the invisible wall and could no longer be seen. This brought a halt to the flow of visitors to Italy.

Mr. Sparkman's son, Robert Sparkman Jr., told us that one of his father's favorite stories was about long-tailed rabbits that lived on Chambers Creek. The story drew inquiries from as far as California, where a rabbit breeder wanted to get some for breeding stock. As a result, plans were formulated by local men to capture a few to exhibit at the Fort Worth Fat Stock Show. The rabbits must have been seen only by their creator, Mr. Sparkman, as they proved to be too wary to be trapped. Although absurd, Mr. Sparkman's tales brought lots of laughs to his readership, as well as stimulating a little interest in the little town of Italy.

In all fairness, it should be written that Mr. Sparkman's hoaxes were not his only legacy! At his death at age seventy-eight, his obituary included an account of his special hobby, which endeared him to thousands of Texans. At his own personal expense he located the graves of scores of Confederate veterans and arranged for the War Department to place appropriate headstones on them. In addition, and perhaps more noteworthy, was his discovery of the long-neglected grave of the mother of two brigadier generals who served

Texas. In 1937 Robert Sparkman discovered the grave of Frances F. Lenoir McCulloch in a remote corner of Ellis County. Mrs. McCulloch had the rare distinction of producing two sons who reached such a high rank. According to the *Handbook of Texas*, one son, Ben McCulloch, came to Texas from Tennessee and joined the army of Sam Houston. He was commander of the two famous cannons, "the Twin Sisters," at the Battle of San Jacinto. Henry McCulloch, one of the twelve children of Frances McCulloch, accompanied his brother Ben to Texas in 1835. He served under Jack Hayes in the Texas Rangers. While serving in the Confederate army he was promoted to brigadier general.

Another of Robert Sparkman's remarkable legacies was the thousands of black walnut trees he caused to be planted throughout Texas and neighboring states as a tribute to servicemen who served in World War II. This time no hoaxer, Sparkman offered through the press to supply walnuts to be planted to grow trees as a tribute to "our boys and men fighting for freedom's cause." Sparkman sent walnuts from an Ellis County tree brought to Texas in 1852. Some of the servicemen were never permitted to return to America. Others returned to thank Sparkman for the idea!

THE LEGEND OF "LANDSLIDE LYNDON" AND THE INFAMOUS BOX 13

From Lyndon B. Johnson's 1948 election to the U.S. Senate until his death, the sobriquet "Landslide Lyndon" hung over his political career like an incongruous comical pall draped over a regal catafalque. Whether or not the epitome of Texas politicians found the alliteration humorous or not is not, to my knowledge, recorded. Nobody, especially Texans, has ever accused Texas politics of being boring or commonplace. While not an integral part of Texas politics, scandal has tarnished the democratic process in Texas on more than one occasion. It probably happens in Texas no more than in any other state, but Texans, as in everything else, seem to do it in grandiose style! But the chicanery in Lyndon B. Johnson's 1948 bid for the U.S. Senate proved to be so unequivocally obvious it is still talked and written about as we speak.

Johnson's road to the White House was virtually assured by his successful Senate campaign against Coke Stevenson. It was that success over fifty years ago that has become a Texas political legend. The legend is best known to Texans as "The Box 13 Mystery." Johnson's nudge into the Senate, and subsequently the White House, was made possible by the tardy (several days after the runoff) report of amended vote totals from the infamous Box 13 in Jim Wells County. The ballot box in voting precinct 13 provided enough votes in Johnson's favor to give him an eighty-seven-vote margin out of about one million votes cast, and the election. Thus he acquired the satirical nickname "Landslide Lyndon." One Dallas newspaper commented on the election as follows: "Many of the voters—listed alphabetically and in the same handwriting—were ineligible, out of the county on election day, or dead." The newspaper reported that LBJ opponents attributed the alleged ballot box stuffing in Jim Wells and surrounding counties to the "Duke of Duval." The late George B. Parr—often dubbed "the emperor of South Texas," and widely considered the last of the state's major political bosses—controlled elections for years in more than a dozen South Texas counties.

TALES OF NATIVE AMERICANS IN TEXAS

When writing about the people of Texas, it would be gross negligence not to include the people who originally inhabited the area that is today Texas. I am afraid that all that some of us know about the North American Indian is the Indian we grew up fighting as youngsters playing "Cowboys and Indians." It will not come as a surprise when we say that the Indians who occupied the land that we call Texas figured prominently in our history; however, there are many facts about these first residents of Texas that are not often written about. We seem to focus our thoughts on the sensationalism offered by the story of the Indian in Texas, and not without reason. They proved to be a formidable force with which our early settlers had to contend. What better venue to write about the culture of our Native brethren that is sometimes overlooked, than in this review of the legends and lore of Texas?

There are some historical facts concerning the Indians of early Texas that we want to share with our readers. Much has been said and written about the early American Indian culture. This is particularly true of their healing practices and methods, many of which were adapted and passed down by early settlers in Texas. We must understand that our white forefathers were in a land strange to them. We must also understand that the Indians' understanding of the healing properties of plants was not their only wisdom about our soil. It is fitting, especially when discussing Texas geography, to look into their agricultural practices. According to the *Handbook of Texas*, "The gardening tribes of Indians had pretty well discovered the western limits of dependable production under primitive methods when Europeans appeared on the scene. Their garden villages at Waco, Village Creek between Dallas and Fort Worth, and on the Red River in Montague County (San Teodora of Spanish records) marked the boundary where corn planting ceased and hunting life began. The border coincides rather closely with the Western Cross Timbers and the thirty inch rainfall line. The East Texas Indians prepared their fields for maize, beans, and squash, by burning off the ground. Seeds were planted with a sharp stick, and the freshly-burned ground required very little cultivation. The shoulder blade of a deer or buffalo served as a hoe for such digging or weed killing as was done. When a plot of ground became unproductive, or weed-infested, a new place was planted, permitting nature to restore the fertility of the depleted plot by the accumulation of plant residues."

Since many Indians have been relegated to scattered reservations across our state, it would, we believe, behoove us to show proper respect and know where these reservations are in Texas. There are: The Alabama-Coushatta, Livingston, Polk County; Tigua, El Paso County; and Kickapoo, south of El Paso.

SURVEYING: A DANGEROUS PROFESSION The Indians' distrust of white folks in Texas, and perhaps elsewhere, made surveying a dangerous profession. Today one does not normally think of the profession as a particularly dangerous one, but this was not the case in the early days of the settling of Texas. According to the 1992–93 *Texas Almanac*, surveyors were hired by homesteaders to locate their land and survey it. Payment for their job and the risk of the job was one-third of the total acreage. And what was the risk involved? Indians recognized surveying equipment and referred to it as "the thing that stole the land," and attacked surveyors whenever possible. It is easy to see why surveyors received "hazardous duty pay." While to us it may sound strange to blame an inanimate object for their loss of land, we must realize that all the Indians knew was that when these instruments appeared, more of their hunting land went away, into the hands of the white man!

An interesting story illustrates just how vulnerable the Indians were to the white man's civilization. It is taken from the book *How Fort Worth Became the Texas-most City*. One was compelled to believe that the American Indian was destined to be totally overcome at the hands of the white man. This book tells us that on December 19th, 1875, Comanche Chief Yellow Bear and his nephew, Quanah Parker, checked into the Pickwick Hotel in Fort Worth, which proudly boasted "artificial gas lights." But this "white man's magic" claimed the life of Chief Yellow Bear. It seems that when the chief and his nephew turned out the gas lights, they failed to close the valve all the way. When they rolled up in their blankets to sleep, Yellow Bear was asphyxiated by the fumes. The fact that he didn't awaken from his slumber wasn't discovered for hours.

One geographical example of how fearful the white man was of the Indians of Texas is the story of "Dead Horse Mountain." Although the Big Bend National Park is visited by many each year, few are aware that the mountains which form its eastern boundary are known locally as "Dead Horse Mountain." Generally called the Sierra del Carmen mountains in Brewster County, the mountains are also known as "Caballo Muerto," which in Spanish means "dead horse." This comes, it is said, from the story that in 1879 a surveying party from Presidio, led by Captain Charles Nevill of the Texas Rangers, killed their worn-out horses rather than let them fall into the hands of Indians.

IT'S PEOPLE THAT TRULY MAKE TEXAS TEXAS!

As we pointed out in the introduction to this section of this book, none of the dramatic events in our state's illustrious history—

none of the state's natural resources—can measure up to the state's most valuable asset, its people! From the larger-than-life heroes of the glorious Texas Revolution, to the uncommon "common men and women" who form the warp and woof of our vibrant red, white, and blue fabric. The people are who have built the mystique that has elevated Texas into world preeminence, and stimulated the pride that the Lone Star State is so famous for.

In this segment of *Texas: Land of Legend and Lore,* we want to lift up on pedestals a few more Texans who have earned special mention in the annals of Texas history. Some of these names you, or your parents, have applauded at one time or another, while we have permitted others to slip into anonymity, and out of our collective mental grasps. We hope that by now, it has become quite evident to the readers of our Texas trivia books how very proud we are of being Texans, and how dedicated we are to publicizing her history, and her culture, from which we Texans spring. It is a heritage of which we can be justly proud! It requires a special breed of stock to produce the hybrid Texans that make up today's population of native Texans. It is fairly easy to look into one's individual family tree, that is, if the tree is native grown, to make a determination as to one's own pedigree. But what about we Texans in a general sense? Those who have gone on before us in the development of the Lone Star State, while individualistic in their contributions, have all exhibited a certain universality that goes, in my opinion, beyond coincidence. It seems that all of the historical characters whom I have researched and written about have reflected the same particular mettle.

No doubt the first settlers brought this characteristic with them to Tejas from their native lands. Those colonists who answered the pleas for adventurers to come to the newly won "Promised land" and stake out a future brought with them their tough-minded spirit, as well as their hard-earned savings, which they invested, sometimes at the rate of as much as 12½ cents an acre, in the well-known "league and labor" of land. For their 12½ cents an acre they got an abundance of cactus (all held together with enough dreams and promises for a bright future, for everyone!). They were certain to be rewarded with more adventures than one could expect in a lifetime somewhere else. It was those who came and stayed that made up the backbone of our pedigree.

Strange as it may seem, and too far-fetched for some of our readers to consider, I sometimes, after reading a description of one of Texas's most prolific and maligned birds, the roadrunner, or chaparral bird, have some reason to believe that native Texans are related to these birds. The description of this bird in the book *Birds of America*, published in 1917, is as follows: "The ground cuckoo or chaparral bird, or roadrunner, is known also as the paisano." The *Handbook of Texas* describes the bird as "one of the most conspicuous and intriguing birds in Texas. The roadrunner, or paisano as he is known to the Mexicans, has a habit of running on the ground to escape its enemies." The book continues, "Its prowess in fighting the rattlesnake is legendary in Texas folklore." Its survivalist spirit permits it to make its way in the most arid parts of the mesquite and chaparral brush-covered parts of Texas. This vivid description of the paisano bird makes it a fitting comparison to Texans when one considers the spirit of those who settled and developed the Texas frontier. Perhaps it is not so unflattering to say that we Texans are a little bit kin to the paisano bird. And are truly "fellow-countrymen" (which is the meaning of paisano).

In addition to our feathered friend, the roadrunner, there are plenty of other examples of the Texans which typify the character and spirit that Texans are made of. Perhaps a review of a few of these would make us all stand a little taller when we see the red, white, and blue of the Texas flag! Fortunately there seems to be enough examples of the stuff Texans are made of to suit all of us, regardless of class, color, or disposition.

JUDGE R. M. "THREE-LEGGED WILLIE" WILLIAMSON AND THE CASE OF COLT VS. BOWIE There are many legends about one of Texas's earliest illustrious characters, and an early proponent of Texas independence—"Three-legged Willie" Williamson. One which writers say depicts Williamson's character best is the legend of *Colt vs. Bowie*. According to the *Handbook of Texas*, "Robert M. Williamson was born in Georgia in 1804. When he was fifteen his schooling was terminated by an illness which left him a cripple for life. His right leg was drawn back at the knee. The wooden leg which he wore from the knee to the ground, resulted in his widely known sobriquet, 'Three-legged Willie.' " Williamson read much during his illness and was admitted to the bar before he was nineteen. He practiced law in Georgia for over a year. He migrated to Texas in 1829. Williamson edited a newspaper for a short time and made an appeal for Texas to resist Mexican tyranny. He was sent to the "Consultation" as a representative, and the government commissioned him a major in 1835, and commissioned him to organize a Ranger company. He participated in the battle of San Jacinto in 1836. The first congress elected him judge of the Third Judicial District. He had a long and eventful political career in Texas history.

"Three-legged Willie" was one of the first non-Rangers to buy a Colt revolver when they became available. One of the legends written about him says that his judicial district included Shelby County, where court had never been held. And when some of the locals heard that court was to be held, they got up a resolution against holding court. The legend says that when it was presented to Judge Williamson, he asked (according to legend), "By whose authority was such a resolution presented?" The presenter, who, like the others who lived in Shelby County, lived by the "law of the Bowie knife," took his Bowie knife, laid it across the resolution, and proclaimed, "This is the law in Shelby County!" "Three-legged Willie" unholstered his Colt, and laying it across the knife, announced, "And this is the constitution that overrides the law. Call the court to order!"

"TEJANOS" While today Texans of Mexican descent are generally called Mexican-Americans, and in some areas of the country, "Chicanos," early Texans of Mexican descent were called "Tejanos." Many Tejanos played important roles in settling Texas and helping her gain her independence from Mexico. A few of our Tejanos were Juan Seguin, Gregario Esparza, and Lorenzo de Zavala. It should be noted that Esparza fought in the Alamo on the side of the Texians, while his brother fought in the same battle on the side of Mexico. Esparza's body was the only defender who was accorded the honor of receiving a Christian burial. All the other defenders were piled up and burned on orders of General Santa Anna.

BESSIE COLEMAN, THE TEXAS BLACK WOMAN WHO MADE AVIATION HISTORY Bessie Coleman, also known as "Queen Bess," was born in 1892 in Atlanta, Texas. She was introduced to airplanes as a child, and she knew that she wanted to fly. She moved to the Chicago area, where she worked in beauty parlors. She had also worked in the cotton fields of Texas. Bessie was unable to find a flying school in America that would accept her as a student because of her race. Hard work and a dogged determination got Bessie to France, where she learned to fly. Bessie got her pilot's license in 1921; this was two years before Amelia Earhart was licensed. "Queen Bess" the barnstormer flew as an entertainer, and was doing what she loved to do best. She was the first African-American woman to be licensed as a pilot.

SCOTT JOPLIN—THE TEXAN WHO PIONEERED A NEW MUSIC GENUS Scott Joplin is another African-American whom we can proudly claim to be on our family tree as a Texan. If you have ever found yourself tapping your toes to the ragtime piano score from the motion picture "The Sting," then you have already been introduced to Texas's Scott Joplin. Once again we rely on the *Handbook of Texas* for our information. Joplin, known as "The King of Ragtime," was born in Texarkana, Texas, November 24, 1868. Coming from a musical family, Joplin learned to improvise on the piano so well that a German musician volunteered to give him piano lessons at no cost. In his early teens, Joplin was an itinerant pianist playing in the "red-light" districts of Texas, Louisiana, and the Mississippi Valley. By 1885, he was playing in the "parlors," the only place open to black musicians in that era in St. Louis (where a primitive sort of music called "jig-piano" was in vogue). The new musical style with the bouncing bass lines and the syncopated melody lines was called "ragged-time," then simply "ragtime."

It is our personal opinion that of all the genes we native Texans have been endowed with, the ones we should all be most proud of are the ones which were provided by the original inhabitants of the vast land called Texas. They are, in our opinion, the most important because they affect not only our relationship of our fellow Texans, but everyone with whom we have contact around the world. These are our "Tejas genes"! Texans pride themselves on being friendly, and some may have lost sight that our state motto is "Friendship." This motto was adopted by the Forty-first State Legislature in February of 1930. It probably was selected because the name Tejas, or Texas, was the Spanish translation of the Caddo Indian word meaning friends, or allies. So our reputation for friendliness not only comes from the attitudes of its citizens, but is well grounded in the history of Texas's first inhabitants. While we may not have the desire or inclination to be explorers or pioneers, and the need no longer exists to show our "bravado" as Indian fighters, we can still exercise our most important inherited genes by making our friendliness more than just a state motto! Regardless of where we go, or what our language differences may be, we can demonstrate exactly what we Texans are made of by letting "Tejas" be our mark of identification!

Chapter Three

LOCAL TRIVIA

One cannot possibly write about the legends and lore of Texas without mentioning some fascinating facts that are not earth-shaking enough to be included in the state's history books! We will use this section of local lore to enlighten and entertain our readers with some of the state's legends not taught in history classes. Often these legends fall through the cracks of teachers' Texas History lesson plans, because they are considered too local in scope!

In this section we will explain why our Texas flag is in such exclusive company, being the only state flag to have served as the standard for an independent nation. According to a North Texas legend, hope springs eternal for childless women who have been bathing in a local fertility spring in hopes of conceiving since the days of the red men. Another bit of local lore reveals how a North Texas oil boom resulted in a nickname being given to a hotel lobby. The sobriquet was attached to the lobby because of the many oil deals consummated there. A bittersweet bit of lore tells how our state had to surrender a champion tree title to Tennessee after our largest pecan tree literally lost its crown!

WERE TEXAS DINOSAURS' HUMAN COMPANIONS FRIENDS OR FRAUDS?

Much has been written about the 100-million-year-old dinosaur tracks discovered in the riverbed of the Paluxy River near Glen Rose, Texas. "The tracks," according to the *Handbook of Texas*, "made by several types of dinosaurs, measure from 12 to 36 inches in length and 9 to 24 inches in width." *Mysteries of the Unexplained*, published by Reader's Digest, shocked us with the revelation that among the Paluxy River dinosaur tracks were found "manlike prints in the same rock stratum—in one case a human print actually overlapped that of a three-toed dinosaur. This is unacceptable to orthodox paleontology, since the giant reptiles were supposedly extinct some sixty million years before man first walked on earth. But the supposition of fraud is based on something more substantial than the simple wish to be rid of objectionable evidence. The refutation of Glen Rose man-tracks rests on the admission that during the Depression a number of local people made money by carving human footprints and selling them as the (real) dinosaur prints. The carving procedure, which involved aging them with acid, was described by the nephew of one of the footprint artists. For those wishing to see an end to the whole improbable story, such admissions were enough to close the case. On the other hand, Mr. Jim Ryals who has said that he and his wife sold prints to tourists, has also stated that they removed several of the human tracks from the Paluxy riverbed using a chisel and a sledge-hammer and then hauling the blocks of rock with a team of horses. Mr. Ryals told investigators how real prints might be distinguished from fakes." The very thought of humans sauntering along with the dinosaurs as they trudged through Central Texas is one of those bits of Texas lore that is truly carved in stone!

TEXAS GHOST TOWNS

Those who create films for our entertainment, especially those who specialize in Western films, have given us, we are afraid, a preconceived idea of what a ghost town consists of. Most of us

This red brick smokestack is the most visible remains of the ghost town of Thurber. The stack was a part of the power plant when the town belonged to the Texas & Pacific Coal Company. The stack was built in 1908. It can be seen from several highways between Ranger and Thurber. Photo from author's collection.

think of a ghost town as a dusty, tumbleweed-strewn, windy street lined with long-abandoned plank structures which were once the nucleus of a Western town, probably of late-nineteenth-century vintage. The lonesome atmosphere may conjure up in our preconditioned minds the certainty that, upon entering any one of the long-abandoned structures, especially (for some unknown reason) the saloon or the long-deserted hotel, we would, given a little time, be confronted by those ghosts of the former residents of the abandoned town. It has become quite easy to let our imaginations run amuck as we turn over in our minds all the scenarios that might have taken place in these buildings. We quickly fall prey to the "If these old walls could only talk" way of thinking. One of the thoughts that is sure to surface in our minds is "What led to the abandonment of the town?" We are using this section of *Texas: Land of Legend and Lore* to assuage our reader's curiosity about some of our state's best-known ghost towns.

THE BREWSTER COUNTY GHOST TOWN OF BOQUILLAS It is, no doubt, because of its Big Bend location and history that Boquillas has all of the ingredients that we believe are required to make a true ghost town! Jim Wheat's book on Texas ghost towns tells us, "This Big Bend town was located in Boquillas Canyon. The discovery of silver and lead ore brought mine promoters, speculators, and immigrants. In 1894 a store was established which was captured by Mexican bandits in 1916. The post office was discontinued in 1906, after the mine closed. After 1940 the village was a trading post with two stores and a population of 30." The *Handbook of Texas* calls it a semi-ghost town at that time. This ghost town is located about twenty miles southeast of Panther Junction on the Rio Grande. Other ghost towns in Brewster County, according to Jim Wheat, are Study Butte, Hot Springs, Glen Springs, and the well-publicized Terlingua. Most of these ghost towns in the Big Bend area were originally developed around mining efforts in the Chisos Mountains, mostly for quicksilver (mercury). The closing of mining operations resulted in the abandoning of the towns. Because of their ambience and histories, it is perhaps easier for us to fall victim to our imaginations, should we visit these towns. We may wander through them with some trepidation! These towns more readily fit the celluloid images we have grown up to associate with the term "ghost town."

One of the examples, in our opinion, of an acknowledged ghost town that is unlikely to be haunted, is located in a much different setting. This Texas ghost town is **the historic port city of Indianola.** Perhaps it is without ghosts of its former residents because little is left of the town to be haunted, unless the ghosts of its settlers, including those hardy German immigrants who were led there by Prince Carl Solms Braunfels, are satisfied residing behind the marker placed there by the state of Texas in 1936. The *Handbook of Texas* tells us, "Of the many ghost towns of Texas, none lived longer, throve better, and none died a more tragic death as Indianola" on the shore of Matagorda Bay, near where René-Robert Cavelier, Sieur de La Salle, is thought to have landed in 1685. Indianola in 1875 had a population of six thousand at the height of its prosperity. In that year the town was struck by a tropical hurricane which took a terrible toll of life and property. Another disastrous tropical hurricane in 1886, caused further loss of life and property. The survivors gave up hope of a revival of trade, and fearing the risk of another hurricane, abandoned the city and moved the county seat to Lavaca, by then called Port Lavaca.

THURBER—POPULATION 5 The town was established in 1886 as a gold-mining town. When the gold became so unproductive that the company could not meet the payroll, the mine was sold to the Texas and Pacific Coal Company. After the discovery of oil in nearby Ranger, the T&P Coal Company was plagued by strikes for higher wages. By this time the town was called "Texas and Pacific Coal." The company had built houses, churches, and schools. Following the strikes the company converted to brickmaking. The company moved to Fort Worth, and the town, having no industry, closed in 1933. The last remaining evidence that Thurber was once an industrial town is the lone tall brick smokestack that can be seen from several highways. In recent years the town has been purchased by a Dallas-area couple, Randy and Andrea Bennett, which has opened the Smokestack Restaurant. At the time of my last visit in 1998, the Bennetts, a family of five, represented the town's entire population. There now are several restaurants in the ghost town of Thurber.

TERLINGUA Perhaps Texas's most publicized ghost town, Terlingua is one ghost town that may have been at one time most susceptible to the spirit world. Thanks to Frank Tolbert and other Texas chiliaficionados, Terlingua has become well known as the most prominent venue for Texas chili cook-offs.

NEARLY TWO THOUSAND MILES OF TEXAS TRIVIA (THE REMARKABLE RIO GRANDE)

The remarkable Rio Grande! This waterway that snakes through one breathtaking canyon after another as it rushes south to empty into the Gulf of Mexico, is far more than a border between Texas and its neighbor to the south! Several of the following facets of Rio

Grande trivia have been exposed individually in our first two Texas trivia books; however, I have elected to string them all together—like pearls on a muddy chain—to present a necklace called, for want of better words, "The Remarkable Rio Grande." You will notice we didn't say "Rio Grande River," as most folks are prone to do! This would, in light of my use of the word "Rio," be redundant, like saying "The Rocky Mountain Mountains." We Texans, unfortunately, tend to think of the Rio Grande as the Rio Grande Valley. While this region has a special place in our heart, there is far more to the river that should not go unnoticed. The 1992–93 *Texas Almanac* is the source of most our material on this, the Daddy of all Texas rivers.

The river is known at different times and at different places along its course by various names, such as "Rio del Norte," "Rio San Buenaventura," "Rio Guanapetuan," "Rio Turbio," and, as in the movies, "Rio Bravo." The name Rio Grande was given the river by the explorer Juan de Ornate, who arrived at its banks at today's El Paso in 1598. From source to mouth, the river drops 12,000 feet to sea level. The length of the river varies, depending on the method of measurement, and its yearly course changes. The latest Water Commission figure is 1,896 miles. Depending on the method of measurement, the Rio Grande is the fourth or fifth longest river in North America. It is Texas's longest river. It irrigates a broad valley of New Mexico dating from the 1600s, the oldest irrigated area in the United States. In the valley above and below El Paso are situated the oldest towns in Texas: Ysleta, Socorro, and San Elizario. Through the Big Bend the Rio Grande flows through three successive canyons: Santa Elena, Mariscal, and Boquillas. The river drains over 40,000 square miles of Texas. Although at first visit it may seem so, the productive and lush green belt that we call the Rio Grande Valley was not always such a paradise! It is said that prior to the early 1900s, when the railroads brought Midwestern farmers who recognized its agricultural potential, only cactus and retama, a thorny shrub, grew in the sandy soil of the Rio Grande Valley.

BELIEVE IT OR NOT! Strange as it may seem, the Rio Grande flows through the Rio Grande Valley at a higher elevation than its surrounding terrain. Over many, many years it has flooded, leaving rich sand deposits and creating a natural levee.

THE RIO GRANDE AS A BORDER The Battle of San Jacinto, which resulted in Texas winning her independence from Mexico, did not result in Mexico giving up her claim to Texas! It seems to have slipped from our memories that it was not until the Treaty of Gaudelupe Hidalgo was signed after the Mexican-American War in 1848, that Mexico relinquished her claim to Texas and the boundary between the United States and Mexico was established as the Rio Grande. Prior to this treaty the Mexicans recognized the Nueces River as the border between Mexico and Texas.

JOHN W. SHARY AND THE RIO GRANDE John W. Shary was known as the father of the Texas citrus industry. He planted the first citrus orchard in the Rio Grande Valley in 1911. The town of Sharyland is named for him.

THE BIG LAND GRAB Previously we mentioned that the oldest towns in Texas were "situated in the Rio Grande Valley." We didn't mention how we came to acquire these historic old towns. According to the *Handbook of Texas* the oldest settlements in Texas are the mission pueblos of Ysleta and Socorro, located near present-day El Paso. They were established in 1682, in Mexico across the Rio Grande from El Paso. These towns remained in Mexico until the flooding of the Rio Grande in the early nineteenth century moved them to the Texas side of the international boundary set by the treaty ending the Mexican-American War. These pueblos were acquired by Texas by a "land grab," assisted by Mother Nature.

OUR SWEET NEIGHBORS ACROSS THE RIO GRANDE As bizarre as it sounds, there was a time when Mexico meant the difference in having or not having that cake or pie! Although we Texans are prone to brag that we have everything, there was a time when we depended upon our neighbor to the south to make it possible for us to have that special pie or cake for dinner. In the mid-1940s, when rationing of sugar was imposed during World War II, it was not so in Mexico! Those living along the Rio Grande in towns having a bridge into Mexico took advantage of our sweet neighbors to the south and trekked across the border, without those coveted rationing coupons, to bring back sugar for those special baked treats.

SETTLING THE RIO GRANDE Our *Handbook of Texas* tells us that José de Escandon, the Spanish colonizer, was responsible for the first successful settlement along the Rio Grande between present-day Laredo and Brownsville. He was born in Soto la Marina in 1700. In 1746 de Escandon was commissioned to inspect the country between Tampico and the San Antonio River, then known as "Seno Mejicano." In January of 1747 he sent seven divisions into the area. In October he presented a colonization plan. Spanish red tape delayed him, but in June 1748, de Escandon was made governor and captain general of Nuevo Sentender. In 1749 he began establishing settlements along the Rio Grande, his first being Carmargo and Reynosa. Only two of de Escandon's permanent settlements were north of the Rio Grande, Laredo and Dolores.

ROBERT E. LEE'S RIO GRANDE CONNECTION I must admit I would never have related Robert E. Lee to Texas, except as it pertained to the Civil War. It was in a conversation with someone who lived at Rio Grande City that his name came up. This prompted me to initiate some research into Robert E. Lee's Texas connection. My research revealed that on March 15, 1860 Lee left San Antonio, Texas for duty at Fort Ringold, located on the Rio Grande at Rio Grande City. His objective was to capture Juan Cortina, the bandit who had opposed General Zachary Taylor in the Mexican-American War. He was an infamous cattle rustler and murderer around Brownsville, Texas. Although experienced in Indian warfare, Lee was unsuccessful in trapping his slippery foe. According to the *Handbook of Texas*, Lee was, however, successful in securing a promise from Mexican officials that they would effect the arrest.

THE TEXAS FLAG IN EXCLUSIVE COMPANY

According to information found in the *Texas Almanac*, "Texas is one of only two states that has a flag that formally served as the flag of an independent nation."

SMALL TEXAS TOWNS AND THEIR UNUSUAL NAMES

In a state that is jam-packed with bigger-than-life heroes, one has little difficulty in understanding why there are so many towns and cities named in their honor! There were 189 patriots at the Alamo alone who committed themselves to die for the cause of liberty for Texians. These sons of the Lone Star State were all destined to have their names immortalized in many ways, including having towns and cities named in their honor. But what about the myriad of small towns we drive through while traversing our great state that have names of questionable origin—towns with names like Dime Box, Dublin, or Post? Unless one is born and raised in these towns of not-so-obvious origin, you are left to wonder how they got their strange handles. There are far too many to consider at just one sitting in front of our IBM, but perhaps we can enlighten you with a few. If you have accumulated a few of your own while traveling in Texas, you are welcome to write to us, and perhaps we can shed some light on them on another occasion.

WESLACO This Rio Grande Valley city was named for **W. E. S**tewart **La**nd **Co**mpany, which promoted the land when the Missouri-Pacific Railroad came through Hidalgo County.

LORENA This Central Texas town was named for a Civil War song that was popular with soldiers on both sides during the war. The city was named by its founder, a railroad executive who was an officer in the Confederate Army. He must have been very fond of the song as he named his daughter Lorena also!

The town of **Buda** (pronounced Byooda) was named for a widow who ran a hotel there. The word is a corruption of the Spanish word viuda, which means "widow."

OLD GLORY Texans are no strangers to patriotism, and this is vividly pointed out in Stonewall County, where the town of Old Glory is located. The original name of the town was New Brandenburg, but anti-German sentiment was so strong in World War I, the citizens changed the name of the town to something more patriotic, hence, "Old Glory."

DIME BOX Among the many Texas legends are those which justify the naming of Texas towns. Legends abound as to how the old town of Dime Box got its name. One legend says there was at one time, in the area where the town was established, a wooden ferry across the river. A rope was stretched across the river at the boat site, allowing anyone wanting to cross the river to pull oneself across the river by boat. There was, according to the legend, a metal box nailed to the tree at the rope site. A sign at the tree instructed the user to "deposit a dime in the box." The community which grew up around this "honor-system" ferry, according to legend, was called "Dime Box." Another legend says that a community existed at the site of today's Dime Box. The residents of this mostly rural community prevailed upon the postmaster, who delivered the mail, to, as a favor, shop for them in town, bringing their purchases with the next mail delivery. The accommodating postmaster, the story goes, put up a metal box in the mercantile store, with instructions that "anyone wanting him to do errands for them should put a dime in the box."

CLYDE Not all Texas towns can boast a pretentious, or romantic, namesake. Such is true of the Callahan County town of Clyde, which sprang up around the construction of the Texas and Pacific Railroad in 1881. The town was named for Robert Clyde, the camp boss of the railroad gang.

One community in Polk County was named in honor of not one, but two, of the town's benefactresses. **Marianna** (originally Drew's Landing) was established in southern Polk County in 1838 by Monroe Drews, who was a trader with the Alabama-Coushatta Indians. A post office was established and given the name of Marianna in honor of Mary and Annie Goodrich, who donated an organ to the town's church.

MERCEDES (What's in a name?) Sometimes a lot more than we think! Although the record reflects that the Rio Grande Valley town of Mercedes was named for Mercedes Díaz, wife of Mexico's president, Porfirio Díaz, there may be more to the name than even its residents know. The town's original name was Lonsboro, after Lon C. Hill, agent and promoter. In 1905 the American Land and Irrigation Company was responsible for its name change. The new name, however, may be more appropriate for other reasons. It is said that in the 1750s, the Spanish Crown gave generous land grants along the Rio Grande to Spaniards of "reliability," meaning wealthy ranchers. According to the *Handbook of Texas,* Mercedes was settled by Mexican ranchers in late 1770 on early land grants. The Spanish grants of the 1750s were called "a merced" (the King's mercy). If the town is situated on one of the old Spanish grants, it is indeed fitting that the new name was selected.

Mobeetie, in Tyler County, was originally named "Sweetwater." When the post office was applied for in 1879, there had to be another name selected as there was already a Sweetwater. The Indian name for sweetwater was selected. A local tongue-in-cheek story says that when the post office pointed out the duplication of "sweetwater," a local Indian was asked to give a name. He gave them Mobeetie. It was learned later that the name meant "buffalo chip." If this tale is true, the old Indian had the last laugh! Authorities tell us that Mobeetie does indeed mean sweetwater.

THE RUSSIAN INFLUENCE ON WEST TEXAS The *Handbook of Texas* tells us that the first immigrants to Ector County found rolling plains covered with mesquite and underbrush. Because of its resemblance to the steppes of Russia, an official of the newly built Texas and Pacific Railroad named the first settlement **Odessa**.

THE TOWN NAMED FOR A WARNING! Once again referring to the *Handbook of Texas*, we learn that **Dublin**, in Erath County, was not named for the Irish capital. The name, originally spelled Doublin in 1860, derives from the warning to wagon trains to "Double In!" (Circle the wagons two abreast!), which alerted them to imminent Indian raids.

Texas has one town in East Texas that had its name changed to benefit local strawberry growers. **Arp**, located in Smith County, was originally named Strawberry. The name was changed to honor William Arp, a popular newspaper editor, and to benefit strawberry shippers who had to hand letter their shipping labels. The shorter name increased the number of crates a shipper could ship each day.

DALLAS'S UPPER-CRUST ADDRESS HAD HISTORIC AND PRIMITIVE BEGINNING

Dallas's fashionable Preston Road, a coveted business and residential address in North Dallas, is given a generous amount of space in the *History of Grayson County, Texas*, published in 1981 by Grayson County Frontier Village, Inc. We are grateful to the publishers for permission to reprint excerpts from that book, including the history of Dallas's Preston Road.

PRESTON OF ROAD FAME LIVED IN DALLAS William G. Preston, the Republic of Texas army captain for whom Preston Road was named, later lived in Dallas County for more than twenty years, and all but two of his twelve children were born and reared here, according to Mrs. Tul V. Rea, a great-granddaughter of the captain. "William Gilwater Preston was born Oct. 15, 1817 in Tennessee," said Mrs. Rea, who has compiled a history of the family. His father was Colonel James Preston, a veteran of the War of 1812, and a friend of fellow Tennessean Sam Houston. Accompanied by his sons, William and George, Col. Preston answered Houston's appeal in 1836 for aid from the United States in Texas's impending struggle for independence. The father and two sons reached the vicinity of San Antonio too late to join the defenders of the Alamo; but all three saw service in the victory at San Jacinto. Col. Preston and his son George returned to Tennessee, but William remained in Texas. In 1840 the twenty-three-year-old William Preston was named captain of a company of Republic of Texas regulars who were stationed in an improvised frontier protection fort on the Red River in what is now Grayson County. It was in the curve of the river which also had a good landing place for crossing the river. The curve in the river became known as Preston Bend, and the settlement that grew up around both was called Preston. In this way the trail, leading some ninety miles southward to John Neely Bryan's town of Dallas, took the name of Preston Road, today State Highway 289.

The ferry and townsite now lie at the bottom of Lake Texoma since the completion of Denison Dam. A marker for Preston Road and the cattle trail that developed on it was dedicated by the Dallas County Historical Survey Committee on the lawn of the Park Cities YMCA. Mrs. Rea and other descendants of Captain Preston were introduced as honored guests.

As the Republic of Texas drew to a close, Captain Preston returned to the United States, enlisting in 1846 for service in the Mexican War in the 1st Arkansas Mounted Volunteers. In 1855 William G. Preston married Sarah Cameron. The couple decided to move to Texas, settling in Dallas County, where Preston bought considerable land at fifty cents an acre. It lay west of the river and adjoined Cockrell's Mountain Creek Plantation.

BLACK-EYED PEAS: A TEXAS NEW YEAR'S TRADITION

When the North invaded the South (Confederate States) during the Civil War, the Southern states being primarily agricultural states, leaders of the North thought they could bring the South down by literally starving it into submission. To facilitate this, Northern troops burned all agricultural crops. Black-eyed peas were a food staple of the South, but the plant was unknown to Yankee troops. Thinking them weeds, the troops failed to put them to the torch. As a result, Southerners were able to sustain themselves on black-eyed peas. To commemorate this stroke of good luck, Southerners started the tradition of beginning each new year by eating black-eyed peas to remind them of their good luck and in hopes the plant would bring them continued good luck throughout the year. This tradition is practiced throughout the South, and as Southerners immigrated to Texas the tradition was brought with them. It was then picked up by the Texans.

TEXAS'S OTHER INTERNATIONAL BORDER

When we think of a Texas river that serves or has served as an international border, our first thoughts are of the Rio Grande. However, one other river has served as an international border on three occasions: The Sabine, which is the 360-mile border between Texas and Louisiana, has served as the international border between the United States and the Republic of Texas, the United States and Mexico, and the United States and Spain.

TEXIANS' LUST FOR LIBERTY CRADLED IN "THE ARMS OF GOD"

One of the most interesting geographical legends in Texas involves the naming of the Brazos River. This poignant legend is accepted by most historians as fact. The legend, as related in the *Handbook of Texas*, is as follows: "The full name of the river, often used in Spanish accounts, is, Brazos de Dios, meaning 'Arms of God.' Many legends have grown up explaining the reason for the name. Probably the earliest is that Francisco Vasquez de Coronado and his men, wandering on the Llano Estacado, were about to perish from thirst when Indians guided them to a small stream which the men named Brazos de Dios, 'Arms of God.' This was subsequently shortened to Brazos, meaning arms."

Although conceived in the hearts of liberty-loving men who had settled Texas as part of Stephen F. Austin's "Old Three Hundred," disenchanted by the actions of the dictatorship established in Mexico by Antonio López de Santa Anna, the gestation of the movement toward independence took place in "the arms of God"! It seems almost providential that so many places relating to the Texians' gaining of independence are located on the river named "The Arms of God." It seems that the almighty, in his wisdom, was cradling these settlers' lust for liberty.

Probably the best-known place relating to the conception of Texas independence is the small town of Washington-on-the-Brazos. This town dates from 1822, when Andrew Robinson began operating a ferry across the Brazos just below the mouth of the

Navasota River. In 1830 Robinson rebuilt the ferry and constructed a tavern, and John W. Hall laid out a townsite on the west side of the river. Several lots were sold but it was not until 1833 that the first residence was built. Hall, Asa Hoxey, and others organized a townsite company and the town was named Washington, probably at the suggestion of Asa Hoxey, who was from Washington, Georgia. The general council of the provincial government met at Washington, as well as the Convention of 1836, which drafted the Declaration of Independence. The town became the capital of Texas in 1842, when the capital was moved from Houston.

"The chicken or the egg?" This age-old riddle is posed here because before there can be a chicken, if we dare use this metaphor in referring to Texas independence, there must be an egg! The "egg," in this context, would have to be another town on the Brazos, San Felipe—actually, San Felipe de Austin. Once again letting the *Handbook of Texas* be our reference, "San Felipe de Austin at the Atascosito crossing of the Brazos River in eastern Austin County is the site chosen by Stephen F. Austin's colonists and the Baron de Bastrop in July of 1823 as headquarters of the colony. San Felipe became the first unofficial capital of all the first Anglo-American settlements." The reference book also points out that "San Felipe also was the site of the conventions of 1832 and 1833, and the Consultation of 1835 met in the town, making it the first capital of the provisional government." Stephen Fuller Austin, "The Father of Texas," lived in the town on the Brazos. Yes! San Felipe was truly one of Texas's most important towns to be nurtured in "the Arms of God"!

THE TEXAS PLEDGE OF ALLEGIANCE

If there is, I'd never heard it until I found it in the *Texas Almanac.* This informative volume tells us that "A pledge to the Texas flag was adopted by the 43rd Legislature. It contained a phrase, "flag of 1836," which inadvertently referred to the David G. Burnet flag instead of the Lone Star Flag adopted in 1839. In 1965 the 59th Legislature changed the pledge to its current form:

"Honor the Texas flag;
I pledge allegiance to thee,
Texas, one and indivisible."

The *Almanac* informs us that "a person reciting the pledge to the state flag, should face the flag, place the right hand over the heart, and remove any easily removable hat."

NEITHER BE BARREN NOR UNFRUITFUL

When Simon Peter used this phrase in writing about Christians in the New Testament scriptures, he was not referring to the fertility of women. There is, however, in Texas a venue that held out hope for those women lacking in the ability to conceive. In our book *A Treasury of Texas Trivia II*, we devoted one section to those places in our state having "unusual claims to fame." As is the case with most efforts outlining the attributes and unusual facts about the Lone Star State, the massive size of the state and diversity of its culture make it easy to overlook material worthy to be included.

Such is the case of Bowie County's "fertility springs." In this far North Texas county there is a place that, according to lore and local beliefs, holds out hope for women desirous of having children, but who have been unable to conceive. If local beliefs are valid, there is no reason for one to expose herself to the risks often associated with fertility drugs. According to Bowie County history, all one needs is to invest in a trip to the little-known community (now practically a ghost town) of Dalby Springs, located about eleven and one-half miles south of De Kalb, Texas. "Archaeological evidence," says the *Handbook of Texas*, "indicates that the spring has been used by prehistoric people for thousands of years. Caddo Indians lived at Dalby Springs before Anglo settlements began in about 1839." The *Handbook* goes on to say that during the 1850s the spring began being known for its medicinal qualities. During the 1870s it is reported that from fifty to seventy people camped out at the springs just to drink the red-colored, foul-tasting water because of its reputation for curing dyspepsia and diseases of the skin and kidneys, as well as female disorders. But by far its most intriguing reputation, which dates back to Indian times, is its remedy for barrenness. Jessie Srygly, a former Bowie County resident, told us that she was told that since the days of the American Indians, women have been known to come to Dalby Springs to drink and bathe in its red-tinted water, having a strong belief in its reproductive powers. So strong is the belief in the spring's power to cure barrenness that someone said that "Had Abraham and Sarah of Old Testament times, come to Dalby Springs, Texas, Isaac would have figured in biblical history fifty years earlier." In his book *Crazy Water*, Gene Fowler wrote extensively about the once sought-after red-tinted waters of Dalby Springs.

LAREDO ... AMERICAN OR MEXICAN?

One of Texas's oldest cities, Laredo, founded in 1755, because of its south-of-the-border ambience, often puzzles first-time visitors. "Is Laredo Mexican or American?" We in the Lone Star State proudly claim Laredo as American. But, believe it or not, there was a time when Laredo was neither American nor Mexican! In the late 1830s and the 1840s, Laredo residents joined the Federalist movement of Northern Mexico, which sought a return to the Mexican Constitution of 1824. The Federalists took up arms against the Centralist government in Mexico City. In 1840 Federalist leaders convened north of the Rio Grande near Zapata or, as some insist, Laredo, declared independence from Mexico, and set up a provisional government for the Republic of the Rio Grande, which included the Mexican states of Tamaulipas, Nuevo León, and Coahuila. The fledgling Republic of the Rio Grande also claimed parts of Texas south of the Nueces River. According to local tradition, the capitol building of the Republic of the Rio Grande was located in Laredo! During these years, Laredo was neither American nor Mexican, but a part of the short-lived Republic of the Rio Grande. The town of Laredo was occupied by Texan troops during the Mexican-American War (1845–1848). At the end of the war the Treaty of Guadalupe Hidalgo firmly established the border between Mexico and the United States as being the Rio Grande and

Laredo became a Texas city. Many Mexican nationals moved south and established the border city of Nuevo (new) Laredo.

DALLAS SUBURB FOUNDED ON SPITE

An article in the *Dallas Morning News* dated April 15, 1996, reporting on Dallas County celebrating its 150th anniversary, includes an interesting fact about Dallas's fast-growing suburb, and the author's residence, Mesquite. According to the newspaper and confirmed by the *Handbook of Texas*, the town was organized as an act of spite by the Texas and Pacific Railroad. The article emphasized the local inhabitants' great attraction to the railroad. "Throughout the county, people, and sometimes whole towns moved to the rails like iron filings are pulled to a magnet. In Scyene—once a separate east Dallas County town, and home of the 'Bandit Queen,' Belle Starr—voters declined to pay a subsidy to the Texas and Pacific for a depot. The railroad punished Scyene by putting the depot in a town it created; Mesquite, which quickly outgrew Scyene." Mesquite was named for nearby Mesquite Creek.

GRAYSON COUNTY'S PECAN TREE BANK

According to the 1981 *History of Grayson County, Texas*, "Grayson County was created by the Texas Legislature in 1846. Its county seat was to be named Sherman after General Sidney Sherman, who is credited with the battle cry 'Remember the Alamo!' The site originally chosen was located about four miles west and some distance north of the present Sherman. The site of the city was later moved to be nearer the center of the county. After the move to new Sherman, Grayson County had no courthouse. A large pecan tree on the courthouse square was used for a courtroom, in addition to being used as a post office, bank, and community center. An old coat was hung on the tree and letters were put in its pockets to be delivered by travelers to other parts of the state. Traders would also hang their saddlebags loaded with gold over the limbs of the tree while they did business in the city.

There is no record of anything being stolen from the 'Pecan tree bank.' Following the destruction of the old county courthouse, there was no place to post public notices. The sheriff propped the door of the dismantled courthouse against the pecan tree and tacked public notices on the door."

HOW THE TOWN OF MEDICINE MOUND GOT ITS NAME

My friend Clem Wills, a product of Hardeman County, brought to my attention that the town of Medicine Mound in Hardeman County got its name from four mounds of earth rising from 200 to 250 feet in height, called medicine mounds. According to the *Handbook of Texas*, "These mounds were Comanche ceremonial sites, and sites for gathering medicinal herbs not found anywhere else." Clem reminded us that folks often incorrectly call the town Medicine Mounds, although there is no *s* on the name. Although there are four mounds, the medicinal herbs gathered by the Indians only grow on one mound.

THE "CHICKEN RANCH" BORDELLO

According to the *Handbook of Texas*, "The Chicken Ranch," a brothel in La Grange, Fayette County, Texas, may have been the oldest continuously running bordello in the nation. Although prostitution started in La Grange as early as 1844, the brothel immortalized in a Broadway musical and movie, "The Best Little Whorehouse in Texas," started after the Civil War when Miss Jessie Williams from Waco bought a small house on the Colorado River. Miss Williams ran a "respectable" house, maintaining a good relationship with the law. She admitted politicians and lawmen, but excluded drunkards! Miss Edna Milton ran the brothel after Miss Williams's death in 1961. It was the onset of the Great Depression of the 1930s that gave the bordello its famous sobriquet. As the economy began to falter, Jessie lowered her prices. As times grew harder, Miss Jessie initiated the "poultry standard": she began to accept chickens for the services of her girls. Soon the place was overrun with chickens, and folks began to call the place "The Chicken Ranch." The brothel ran continuously until mid-1973, when consumer affairs reporter Marvin Zindler of TV station KTRK in Houston ran an extensive exposé on the brothel.

DID YOU EVER WONDER IF TEXAS EVER BRAGS ABOUT ANYTHING SMALL?

You bet your boots it does! While folks think everything in Texas is "bigger, and better," there are many small things in the Lone Star State that are mighty hard to beat! We have previously written about "The Littlest Skyscraper" found in Wichita Falls, but thanks to the Texas Parks and Wildlife Department, we can brag about our state's smallest state park! The **Acton State Historical Site**, at .01 acre, or twelve feet by twelve feet, is Texas's smallest state park. Located in Hood County, the park is the burial site of Davy Crockett's second wife, Elizabeth. She married the Texas hero in Tennessee in 1815. She died January 31, 1860. Since Crockett fought for Texas and died at the Alamo, his heirs were eligible for a land grant, but Mrs. Elizabeth Crockett did not claim her grant until 1853. By that time all choice land had been claimed and she had to give the surveyor half of her land for locating a tract worth claiming. The land was in northeast Hood County near Acton. To reach the Acton Cemetery go 4.5 miles east of Granbury on US 377 to FM 167 south, then 2.4 miles south on 167 to Acton. The cemetery will be on the right.

ARE YOU AN EX-TEX OKIE?

If you lived in Greer County, Texas between February 8, 1860 and 1906, you are a member of a very exclusive fraternity! You are an Ex-Tex Okie. Greer County was formed February 8, 1860, with the town of Mangum selected as its county seat. A border dispute which found itself in the United States Supreme Court resulted in a verdict ceding this entire county, consisting of one and a half million acres of land, to Oklahoma. In 1906, what had been Greer

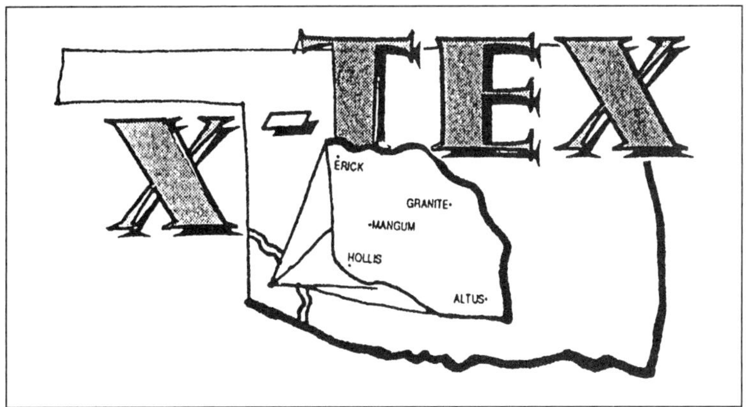

This map, showing the southwest corner of the state of Oklahoma, indicates the location of what in 1860 was Greer County, Texas. This entire county was lost to Oklahoma as a result of a U.S. Supreme Court ruling in a border dispute.

County, Texas became a part of the state of Oklahoma, making its former residents "Ex-Texas Okies." On March 16, 2006, this region of Oklahoma will be able to celebrate the 100th anniversary of its "liberation" from Texas! We are indebted to Krin Boswell of Ninnekah, Oklahoma for providing this truly forgotten footnote to Texas history.

BURY ME NOT ON THE LONE PRAIRIE (INSPIRATION FOR COWBOY SONG FOUND IN ARCHER COUNTY, TEXAS?)

In his book *Trails Through Archer*, author Jack Loftin has included a bit of Texas lore that poignantly reflects the life of the Texas cowhand, and Loftin has generously permitted us to reprint this cowboy lore in this volume. "For years there has been a grave on the banks of the South Fork of the Little Wichita River and east line of Block 104 Harris subdivision. On the sandstone is inscribed 'J. Giddin 1876.' This grave was first discovered in the year 1879, about the time of the organization of the county. And it was thought that it was the grave of some buffalo hunter. This came to be the general opinion of all, in speaking of it. But in 1889 a crowd of young people, who were strolling along the banks of the river, found the grave. Looking around they found a sandstone marker with something carved thereon, but the name was too dim to decipher. They made out the words 'cowboy' and 'last words.' It was thought that this was some cowboy that had been with some passing herd and had taken sick and died, or was shot, or had other misfortune; his comrades had buried him in this lonely grave and carved on the sandstone his name and last request. The words that could be made out, said some of the old-timers, corresponded to those in the poem, 'The Dying Cowboy.' It was thought that this grave or this cowboy might have been the inspiration for the writer to have composed the well known cowboy ballad, 'Oh bury me not on the Lone Prairie.' We reprint the words for those who may not have heard it and for those who may have often visited the grave and read the words on the sandstone which furnish the only clue as to who is buried in this lonely and unknown grave. The best conclusion," says Loftin, "is that the man drowned while crossing the river with cattle, when his horse bolted. This was recently uncovered in an interview with a man who had worked with Jim Scott as a cowboy in the area. Scott would have been in the county about the time of the cowboy's death. The grave of this unknown lies just a half mile southwest of Spring Mountain on the east bank of the South Fork of the Little Wichita River on the lands of C. L. Abercrombie, three miles west of Archer City."

"The Dying Cowboy"

Oh bury me not on the lone prairie
These words came low and mournfully
From the pallid lips of the youth who lay
On his dying bed at the close of day
He had wailed in pain till o'er his brow
Death's shadows fast were gathering now;
He thought of his home and his loved neigh
As the cowboys gathered to see him die.

Oh bury me not on the lone prairie
Where the wild coyotes will howl o'er me
In a narrow grave just six by three
Oh bury me not on the lone prairie.

WHATEVER HAPPENED TO THE DALLAS COUNTY TOWN OF LISBON?

Lisbon, according to the *Handbook of Texas*, in south central Dallas County between Dallas and Lancaster, was named for Elizabeth Williamson, a pioneer hotel owner. A post office was granted in 1880, with J. G. Williamson serving as postmaster. The population was 140 in 1910 and 300 in 1930. The early town of

This is the first home built in the "lost" Dallas County town of Lisbon. It was built by the three Sloan brothers. Known as the Samuel Sloan cabin, the "dog-trot" cabin was donated to Northwood University where it serves as an office. The cabin was moved to the University campus and restored in 1984–1985. The Sloan cabin is a perfect example of the "dog-trot" style cabins built by many early Texas settlers. This photo was made by Craig Root and is furnished by Northwood University. Like other early Dallas County towns, Lisbon was absorbed into the rapidly growing city limits of Dallas.

Lisbon is probably remembered by most of us with Dallas roots as the location of the U.S. Veterans Administration Hospital. We can remember when Dallas Railway and Terminal served Lisbon and south Oak Cliff with a bus marked "Lisbon." In a conversation with Helen Anthony, who grew up in Lisbon and who is the author of the book *Lisbon West of the Trinity*, we were provided with a valuable and knowledgeable overview of the town's history and character. First of all, Mrs. Anthony, who has obviously researched this former Dallas County town, takes issue with the usually reliable *Handbook*'s version of how the town got its name. She can offer no proven explanation, based upon her research, to support Elizabeth Williamson as the town's namesake. This aspect of the town's history is not important to its being recognized as a town "Lost in the shuffle"!

Let us first establish the town's location. The heart of the earlier town was, according to Mrs. Anthony, the crossroads of what is, today, Ann Arbor and Lancaster Road in the south Oak Cliff section of Dallas. Lisbon was situated on a land grant awarded to the Sloan Brothers, Robert and Samuel and a third brother, for their service in fighting in the Texas Revolution. In 1838 Robert surveyed a road in North Texas. James Sloan brought his family to Texas under a Peters Colony grant. Mrs. Anthony said that Lisbon was once known as "Old Virginia." This will be as much a surprise to many as it was to me. The reason for the name is unknown, but, as was often the case, the naming of a town could be based on a settler's home town or state.

Lisbon Cemetery, in which a number of old settlers are at rest, is located near Denly Drive and Ann Arbor on land given by the Sloan and Gracey families. Both families were prominent during the span of one hundred years in Oak Cliff. The Veterans Hospital sits on Sloan land which was sold to a family in Lancaster and purchased by the U.S. government. Lisbon Elementary School, located at 4203 South Lancaster, is in use today by the Dallas Independent School District as an elementary school. It sits on the site of the original Lisbon school, which originally served as a combination church and school in the old days of Lisbon. The original school burned in 1922. The old Sloan "dog-trot" cabin can be seen today on the campus of Northwood University, where it is used as an office. Our visit to this historic Dallas County log cabin was at a season when the surrounding woodland was awash with dogwood blooms. The scene gave us a good idea of what this part of Dallas County looked like in the days of the pioneers. The cabin was donated to the university by the heirs of the Sloan family.

Mrs. Anthony reflected great disappointment that DART had demolished some of the precious few original structures from Lisbon to build its rail lines. In reflecting on early transportation in Lisbon, Mrs. Anthony recalled how folks who worked in Dallas rode the Texas Electric Interurban, which ran both north and south and could be boarded in Lisbon. She also reminisced about another mode of transportation to and from Lisbon, called a "jitney." Her use of this infrequently heard word forced some additional research. Mrs. Anthony said that the "jitney" of her days "was a Model T Ford and the fare was a nickel." My research showed that "jitney" came from the French word "jeton," meaning token, about 1903. It meant "a small car or bus that carries passengers for a low fare, originally five cents." Mrs. Anthony emphasized that if there were too many passengers, some would ride on the running board. Lisbon was "lost in the shuffle" in 1929 when it was annexed into the City of Dallas.

ST. MARTIN CHURCH ("SMALLEST ACTIVE CATHOLIC CHURCH IN THE WORLD")

When one writes about a state that has a reputation for bigness, the smallest anything sticks out like the proverbial "sore thumb." We read that a journey to the heartland of German and Czech settlers in Central Texas would yield what has been called "The smallest active Catholic Church in the world"; it sent our investigative juices into overdrive. The discovery of the tiny St. Martin Catholic Church in the town of Warrington in picturesque Fayette County demanded detailed information. Kathy Madere at the nearby Round Top Library graciously furnished us with a copy of Norman C. Krishchke's book *St. Martin Church*, which filled in the blanks to our many unanswered questions. We are grateful to the author for permitting us to use excerpts from his book so that this Texas "smallest" is better understood. Mr. Krischke explains that "There were scores of Catholic families living in the Warrington area before 1886 who did not have access to the sacraments other than at Fayetteville. Father Joseph Chromcik organized a congregation there in 1886." In 1888 an acre of land was acquired and St. Martin Church and Cemetery were established in 1888 and 1889. A church sixty-eight feet by thirty-six feet was erected. Krischke tells us that a parochial school was needed in Fayetteville, and on July 15, 1915, the Bishop in Galveston gave permission to demolish St. Martin Church and use the lumber for the large two-story school. In 1936 the school was demolished and a smaller school constructed from the salvaged lumber. The small school building was demolished in 1968 to make room for parking spaces for a new brick church. In 1915 there was enough lumber left over from the school project to build the small chapel at the original site of St. Martin Church. This small chapel is called "The smallest active Catholic Church in the world." The building is fourteen feet, three inches by eighteen feet, one inch. It contains some of the fixtures, including the altar and tabernacle, and statues from the original St. Martin's. It has twelve wooden benches built in as pews, which will seat about twenty people. Tiny as this Texas church is, it still sports a steeple and bell.

LUFKIN LORE PROVES EAST TEXANS CAN'T BE TRIFLED WITH!

One of the many examples of lore that comes from the deep East Texas piney woods, a region that is a breeding ground for lore, is the story about how the city of Lufkin was founded. If one can believe tradition, the East Texas timber capital of Lufkin was born out of one man's revenge. Tradition has it that in 1876, Homer was the county seat of Angelina County, and Lufkin did not exist. Homer's seat of importance was, however, doomed because of its intolerance of rowdies! During the construction of the Houston East and West Texas Railroad, known locally as "the rabbit" through the piney woods of East Texas, the HE&WT steel crew, who earned a wage of two dollars a day for their backbreaking work, were hard at work laying track through Angelina County when an incident occurred which would change the complexion of the county! As could be expected, on payday, they went into Homer to "let off steam." When they became drunk and, no doubt, rowdy, Sheriff W. B. "Buck" Green, according to the legend, threw the whole bunch in the hoosegow. The survey boss, Edwin P. Lufkin, went to town to bail them out. He was so enraged by Homer's lack of hospitality that he refused to lay the tracks through the town. This decision meant finis for the town of Homer. The tracks were laid seven miles west of Homer, where a new town was laid out, which was named Lufkin. Paul Bremond, a Houston financier who started the railroad in the mid-1870s, divided the site into lots and put on a big real estate promotion. In a reasonably short time Lufkin became a thriving city. After the courthouse in Homer burned in 1891, Lufkin, the city born out of revenge, became the county seat of Angelina County.

AUSTIN ONCE ILLUMINATED BY ARTIFICIAL MOONLIGHT

The *Handbook of Texas* tells the complete story of the 165-foot-tall so-called "Moonlight (or moon) towers" that once served to illuminate the capital city of Austin, Texas. The so-called "Moonlight (or moon) towers" in Austin are the only surviving examples of the tower lighting systems that were common in American cities in the late 1800s. The towers, erected in 1894 and 1895, were fabricated by the Fort Wayne Electric Company and shipped in pieces to Austin. The original installation contract included electric generators installed at Austin Dam on the Colorado River. During their early years the towers were equipped with carbon-arc lamps that diffused light over a large area. In 1925 the towers were converted to incandescent lamps and in 1936 to mercury-vapor lamps. The *Austin Daily Statesman* reported that a newspaper could be read by the light from one of the 165-foot-tall towers at a distance of 1,500 feet.

The lights have remained in nearly continuous operation for over one hundred years. They have been turned off only twice.

This photo shows one of Austin's remaining "moonlight" or moon towers erected in that city in 1894–1895, and was one of the towers that gave our capital the reputation of being lighted by "artificial moonlight"! Photo by David Thomason of the Texas Association of Homes and Services for the Aged, in Austin.

They were off for one week in 1905 because of a dispute between the City Council and the Water and Light Commission. In 1973, they were off briefly in response to a national energy crisis. Of the original thirty-one erected, in the early 1900s seventeen still stood, most of them in old residential neighborhoods near downtown. In 1970 the towers were designated official state archeological landmarks, and by 1976 they had been added to the National Register of Historic Places. During the early 1990s the City of Austin undertook a comprehensive restoration program, taking each of the towers down and sandblasting, repairing, and repainting it, then replacing it on its original site. With seventeen of the towers still in operation, Austin is the only city that has retained these charming reminders of an age gone by.

HAVE YOU EVER WONDERED WHY WAXAHACHI'S BEAUTIFUL OLD COURTHOUSE HAD SUCH UGLY FACES CARVED ON ITS FAÇADE?

Many Texas courthouses and other old buildings are of the architectural style that includes the grotesque faces of gargoyles, but not so with the much acclaimed Ellis County courthouse at "Cow Creek," or Waxahachi. The noticeable ugly faces carved into the façade of this beautiful and historic old seat of county government are the source of one of Texas's most bizarre legends. Although we have written about this town with its myriad of beautiful Victorian homes, and its haunted restaurant, on more than one occasion, we want to assuage the curiosity of those who have seen this stately courthouse and have wondered about the faces carved in the red stone above its pillars.

Few towns north of San Antonio, with its history steeped in the history of the Texas Revolution, have received as much publicity as the Ellis County town of Waxahachi. The name, according to the *Handbook of Texas*, comes from an Indian word meaning "cow, or buffalo creek." The town, founded in 1846, is probably best known for its beautiful, 100-year-old county courthouse, built in 1895. Replete with battlements and turrets, the

Although the Ellis County Courthouse in Waxahachi is recognized as one of the state's most photogenic seats of county government, the Waxahachi courthouse is perhaps best known for the legend of the grotesque facial carvings seen on its portals. Pictured here are some examples of the work of the Italian stone carver whose flirtatious advances were spurned by a local lady.

courthouse was featured in James Michener's book *Texas*. In his book Michener told the legend of the faces carved in stone. He told how the building is famous for its tale of a spurned love affair. Legend has it that an Italian stone carver, hired to carve the courthouse columns, boarded with the Frame family. He fell in love with the family's daughter, Mable. He chiseled her image on the courthouse façade. Mable spurned his affections but the rejected suitor continued to carve her face repeatedly, making it progressively uglier! These faces can be seen today on the borders of the portals at each entrance to the courthouse.

Perhaps as famous as the beautiful granite courthouse are the town's Victorian homes that are generously sprinkled throughout the town. Local publicists proudly proclaim that there are more turn-of-the-century homes on the national and state historical register in Waxahachi than can be found in any other town in Texas. It was in one of these Victorian homes, built in 1895, that Marianne and I discovered Waxahachi's popular haunted restaurant, The Catfish Plantation. In addition to its reputation of being home to ethereal visitors, the beautiful old house has an attraction to sports fans. Located at 814 Water Street, this restaurant was the birthplace of Major League Baseball great Paul Richards, who managed the Baltimore Orioles and the Chicago White Sox. His prowess as a young pitcher was chronicled in the December 6th, 1987 edition of the *Dallas Morning News*, reporting how the "Waxahachi-born hurler made Ripley's Believe-It-or-Not column by pitching a shutout left-handed to lead his Waxahachi High School team in the state semifinals, only to pitch right-handed the next day to win the state championship." The baseball player's home-turned-catfish-restaurant has achieved notoriety as a haunted house. Restaurant owner Melissa Baker told us that the professional "Ghostbusters" brought in to evaluate the unnatural happenings experienced by employees, including flying coffee cups and appearances of ghostly figures, identified three deceased people connected with the old Richardson home who were making the disconcerting returns to the old house. One ghost had died on her wedding day in 1920. Although the haunted restaurant may not quite measure up to the legend of the town's faces carved in stone, it is still another of Texas's interesting bits of lore that make our cities, towns, and villages so attractive to visitors.

LIVING ON THE SOUTH BANK OF THE "BIG RED" MAKES YOU AN OKIE

The Treaty of Guadalupe Hidalgo, which ended the Mexican-American War (1846–1848), provided that the border between the United States and Mexico would follow the main channel of the Rio Grande, which divided ownership of the river between Texas and Mexico. Not so with the Texas border between Texas and Oklahoma, the Red River. In March of 1896 the Supreme Court ruled that the

Oklahoma state line extends to the south bank of the Red River, making the Red River the sole property of Oklahoma.

TIOGA, HOME OF GENE AUTRY AND ANOTHER TINY TEXAS JAIL

The North Texas town of Tioga would have been called Autry, Gene Autry, or possibly Autryville, if the famous singing cowboy had been given his way, but thanks to physician Dr. Eugene Ledbetter, who brought the future recording and Western film star into the world, the town's Indian name stayed the same. Miffed because the family had not paid for Autry's delivery fee, the doctor, who was one of the town's city fathers, talked down the name change, which was requested by the star in return for his help in bolstering the town during its economic slump. The town did, however, name a street for the singing cowboy.

The star who was given his doctor's first name, Gene Autry, is not the only historical feature in this town that once was a popular health spa. If one tours this friendly little Grayson County town and keeps a sharp eye, they just might spot a sure runner-up in our search for Texas's tiniest jail. Grapevine's little "calaboose" is a shoo-in for first place in the category of "tiny Texas hoosegows," but in Tioga a small red brick building that might be mistaken for a custom-made garage for a Volkswagen beetle, is actually the town's City Jail. A sign informs us that the jail was built in 1900. The dwarf pokey sits under a large, gnarled bois d'arc tree that, by its size, appears, like the old jail, to be a centenarian. The pastoral setting of this friendly, picturesque North Texas town does not reflect the need for a bastille of any size. The town, founded by the T&P Railroad in 1881, must have felt the need for at least some semblance of law and order, which resulted in the construction of this antiquated City Jail. The brick structure is ten feet wide by twelve feet deep and has a tin roof and a cement floor. It has an iron or steel door that is grated so you can see in or out. Each of its three windows, measuring eight by eighteen inches, is barred. There are no furnishings in the jail except for a single steel ring imbedded in the cement floor, to which chains could be attached, which could hardly be called a furnishing. The small jail, a stark reminder of the harshness of days gone by in Texas, loudly screams the message, "Crime doesn't pay!"

The dwarf calaboose was last used, I learned, in the mid-1940s when the Tioga city Marshall was Charles (Uncle Charlie) Nicholson. In a conversation with Charlene Brown, I learned that her father, Otis Renfro, operated a service station and garage in the vicinity of the old jail. The Marshall, like other men, often hung out at the station. Mrs. Brown related that many local farmers traded with her Dad. One day a farmer rushed in saying that a "Negra" [*sic*] showed up at a farm house and "was all bloody." He had a knife and when questioned about his condition contended that he had been killing hogs. The man reporting the incident wanted Marshall Nicholson to come out to the house as the farmers were scared! "Uncle Charlie" didn't have a car so Mrs. Brown's father, who had a black car, a Mr. Scoggins, and the city Marshall went to arrest the man until they could find out more about him. The three men brought the black man back to the Tioga city jail. The jail, Mrs. Brown said, had to be emptied of bales of hay being stored in it before the prisoner could be locked up. Mrs. Brown told how frightened she and her sister were upon seeing the man. Calls were placed to the sheriff in Sherman and the Texas Rangers were called to see if the man was wanted. The city Marshall found out that lawmen had been frantically searching for the man who was accused of attacking a couple of college students from Denton, raping the woman and stabbing her male friend. This, said Mrs. Brown, was the last time the red brick jail had been used.

OIL BOOM GIVES HOTEL LOBBY A NICKNAME

The discovery of oil in the Burkburnett region of Wichita County, Texas in the early 1900s was responsible for the economic development of much of that county, including Wichita Falls. One of the city's best-known hotels, the Kemp, was a direct result of the oil boom. In Louise Kelley's book *Wichita County Beginnings*, the author, in speaking of the Kemp, tells us, "The lobby was usually filled with oil men and the spill over stood outside against the wall." It is implied that many oil-related deals were consummated in the lobby. The lobby's reputation as "the place to wheel and deal in the oil industry" was responsible for the lobby of the Kemp being given the nickname, "Lobby Drilling Company."

GRAYSON COUNTY'S JAIL ON WHEELS

In Vol. II of the *History of Grayson County, Texas,* there is a history of Grayson County's jail on wheels, officially known as "The Work Camp Jail." At first glance, says the history, it might have been mistaken for an animal cage on wheels, but its height, with walls of cross-barred steel, suggested something more. It was built as a holding prison for men. Its height was to allow for two floors. The wagon had an upper and lower floor. There was space to hold thirty prisoners. One Sherman, Texas woman reported in the history that in 1904 or 1905, she watched a chain gang work on her street, then a country road. This was before this practice was stopped in 1931. "The chain," she said, "consisted of about a dozen men, all black. Each had a chain about ten feet long shackled to his ankle. At the end of the chain was an iron ball, about the size of a bowling ball. As the men moved along," she continued, "they carried the ball with them or dragged it to a location and worked as far as the ten feet would allow. A short distance away," the woman related, "I could see a two-tiered cage on wheels, in which the men had been transported to the work site. When the weather permitted, the men lived, ate, and slept, as long as they worked at that location." This jail on wheels, officially known as the "work camp jail," can be seen at Sherman's Loy Park.

TEXAS'S SMALLEST JAIL

Although I have not visited every jail in Texas, either as a guest or professionally, I am convinced that, after reading this, you will agree that Grapevine's "Cross-bar Hotel" will easily qualify as our state's smallest jail. This trivia item is not meant to be a soapbox

Built in 1909, this tiny, sparsely appointed calaboose served to cool off many a hot-headed cowboy in Grapevine, Texas. Few Texas hoosegows can compete with this city jail in a contest for the state's smallest jail. Photo by Bill Binnig.

on which to climb and spout our personal philosophy, or render personal opinions on the care and feeding of those miscreants who, because of their own misdeeds, find themselves incarcerated in the jails or prisons in Texas! We do hope, however that those "Do-Gooders" who file lawsuits on behalf of prisoners who have been "deprived of color television," or have been "forced to eat crunchy peanut butter, instead of their preferred smooth," will take note of the living conditions of those who ran afoul of the law in Grapevine after 1909! Sallie Andrews of the Grapevine Heritage Foundation sent us a fact sheet on that city's 95-year-old "Calaboose." The term "calaboose" comes from the Mexican slang word for jail, "calabozo." This interesting old relic of the city's past is, perhaps, the crown jewel of Grapevine's historic Main Street district. Before the building of the Calaboose, the city of Grapevine had relied on the Tarrant County Sheriff to provide law enforcement. In June of 1909 the town council voted unanimously to build the community's first calaboose. The Council gave town Marshall W. T. Bigbee authorization to build the eight-by-ten-by-eight-foot concrete jail. The fact sheet goes on to say that in the same meeting, Marshall Bigbee was given $4.50 for the purchase of a pair of handcuffs. "It is supposed," said the fact sheet, "that Bigbee had his own gun at the time." The Marshall was offered $25.00 a month at the time. The calaboose wasn't used much after 1953 to house prisoners. This "home-away-from-home" for those who ran afoul of the law in Grapevine offered little in the way of comfort. If its cramped size is not enough to be convincing of its being bereft of comfort, the fact sheet tells us that "The single iron cot and the tarp thrown over the openings to keep out the chilly wind, were no longer adequate to contain the occasional inebriated citizen, so the jail fell into ruin." No doubt the Grapevine Calaboose cooled off many a rowdy cowboy in its day!

DID YOU EVER WONDER WHY DAMSITE IS NOT A NAUGHTY WORD IN TEXAS?

Clemmie Wills, who previously resided in Hardeman County on the Red River, related to me the story of how the North Texas town of Damsite got its unusual name. It seems the Rice Brothers had extensive land holdings in Hardeman County and when they decided to dam up Wanderer's creek that created what is now Lake Pauline, while looking over the proposed project one of the brothers is said to have commented, "Now that's a dam site!" As a result, the town that grew out of the work camp for building the dam in the early 1920s was called Damsite. The motto of the town's promoters was "Best town in Texas, by a damsite!"

WHICH DENOMINATION OF AMERICAN CURRENCY HAS TEXAS ENGRAVED ON IT?

The back side of the five-dollar bill pictures an engraving of the Lincoln Memorial. In the border above the columns one can, aided by a magnifying glass, find the word TEXAS engraved. It can be located almost directly over the fourth column from the left.

Officials at the memorial tell us that those states in existence at the time the memorial was built in 1922 are engraved on the façade of the memorial. From left to right one can read Arkansas, Michigan, Florida, and Texas.

HOW HUSHPUPPIES GOT THEIR NAME

If you've ever wondered how the tasty cornmeal balls, usually deep fried and served with fish dinners, got their name, this bit of trivia should be a revelation.

Although undocumented, one Texas legend, which has the ring of truth, tells us that in the days of Texas cotton plantations, the open doors of the houses, both the Master's house and those of the slave quarters, made it easy for the family dogs to accept the invitation issued by the kitchen aromas at mealtime. Once inside, the pups would make their way under the dining table, where they would whine noisily until a sympathetic or aggravated family member slipped them a morsel of table food. Once satisfied, the dogs would ease out from under the table and return to the outside environs. It is said that in order to placate the whining dogs and expedite their departure so the family could finish their meal in peace, the Negro mammy who cooked for the family would make up a batch of cornmeal dough seasoned with meat grease, and, after portioning the dough in little balls, deep-fry it and put it on the table as puppy pacifiers. When the dogs whined, the tasty pacifiers were slipped to the dogs with a friendly command, "Hush puppy!"

KILGORE'S "TROTLINE BAPTIST CHURCH"

Kent Biffle's "Texana" column in the *Dallas Morning News* revealed a segment of the great East Texas oil boom's history that we had never written about. While the 1930s oil boom in Kilgore had brought instant riches to many, and increased population to a town that had been so quiet it didn't even have a jail, it also spawned a crime wave to equal its economic explosion. There was an immediate influx of swindlers, pimps, prostitutes, and all the other vermin usually attracted by the smell of easy money! Biffle writes, "Cops were underpaid and overwhelmed! Now and then six or seven Rangers rode in to keep the lid on. The one everybody talked about was, of course, 'Lone Wolf.' Wearing a tailored suit, a pair of pearl-handle six guns, and an Ipana smile, Ranger Sgt. Manuel Trazasas (Lone Wolf) Gonzaullas bedazzled Kilgore." He ran a heavy chain the length of an abandoned church house. He attached short chains to the long one. He tethered the short chains around the necks of the offenders that were his "catch-of-the-day." This old church became known as the "Trotline Baptist Church."

DID YOU EVER WONDER HOW THE TOWN OF CUT AND SHOOT GOT ITS NAME?

The naming of this South Texas town, located forty miles north of Houston, according to the *Handbook of Texas*, came, unfortunately, as a result of a church dispute. Disputes have historically resulted in divisions of churches. But in the case of Cut and Shoot, the dispute, which is also unclear, gave the town its name. There are, says the *Handbook of Texas*, three versions of the controversy among the members of the town's only church. One version is there was a dispute over the design of the church's steeple, while another says the disputation was over who was going to preach there. Still another claim is that the dispute was a land claim among the church's members. What seems to be certain is that during the dispute, a young boy declared, "I'm going to cut around the corner and shoot through the bushes." The boy's phrase remained in the residents' minds and was eventually adopted as the town's name. We are grateful to the *Handbook of Texas* for the insight into the unusual name of this Texas town, which takes its place among other Texas towns with strange names, like Bug Tussle, Toadsuck, and Gun Barrel City.

"JERK-WATER" TOWNS

The dictionary defines the term "jerk-water" as meaning "small, unimportant, etc., often a small town." Perhaps some of our readers have been born in, or lived in, a very small town, which was referred to by some as a "jerk-water" town? We feel that considering the historical origin of the term "jerk-water," this would be a topic worthy of a few column inches in this book of legend and lore. It might be a balm to to anyone who has taken umbrage at this terminology in describing their place of birth or residence. So, before anyone has their feelings hurt, or feels insulted by this demeaning term, we think that you will feel better if you are made aware of the origin of the term. It has a much more historical background than one might think. If your family has roots in early railroading, especially in Texas, you may already know that a "jerk-water" town is not as derogatory a term as you always thought!

For clarification of the origin of the term, we went to *Morris's Dictionary of Word and Phrase Origins*, and to Bob LaPrelle, Director of the Age of Steam Museum at Dallas's Fair Park. From these sources we learned that the word, with its origin in early railroading, is not directed toward small towns in Texas alone. No! Based upon its origin, we learned that there are probably more "jerk-water" towns north of the Mason-Dixon line. First we must point out that in the days of steam locomotives, the trains had to take on water for making steam about every one hundred miles. The water was stored in a tender car behind the locomotive. Northern lines such as the New York Central were very competitive and tried not to stop any longer than necessary to maintain their schedule. Some of these lines featured locomotives with scoops on the tenders which, we were told, allowed the locomotives to slow to about forty-five miles per hour, at which time the scoops could be lowered as the train passed over a trough which had been installed between the tracks, and which was kept full of water from a storage tank. The scoop literally jerked the water into the tender. Railroad employees were required to be housed at the location of these troughs to maintain the tanks and watering facilities. There was, in most cases, little else of importance to be found at these towns. They were, for obvious reasons, called "jerk-water" towns.

In Texas, as a general rule, our source told us, the same need existed, but a slightly different method was used to keep the water tenders filled. Water towers or standing tanks were constructed at various locations along a stretch of railroad line. The train would stop momentarily under an enormous spigot, which was attached to the water towers. The fireman would jerk a cord that would release the water from the tower and allow it to to flow through the spigot and into the tender behind the locomotive. Once again, often a small community grew up around the railroad watering facility. These small communities were called "jerk-water" towns. So, based upon the information furnished us, those small unimportant towns that we today sometimes call "jerk-water" towns, grew out of an important phase of our development, the railroads. If one truly has roots in such a town, one can take pride, rather than take exception, to being from a "jerk-water" town!

One example of a Texas town that originated from a "jerk-water" town is the Brewster County seat of Alpine. A brief history of this beautiful Big Bend town, and its relationship with the railroad, was found in the August 15, 1968 edition of the *Alpine Avalanche*, which, along with the book *Alpine, Texas, Then and Now* by Doctor Clifford B. Casey, provided us with a deeper insight into the development of Alpine, as it related to the Southern Pacific Railroad's need for water. The following excerpts are reprinted by permission of the archives of the Big Bend Library at Sul Ross University. Herbert L. Kokernot, in speaking of part of this land, told the *Avalanche*, "There were no springs on the property that he knew of, but recalled that the Southern Pacific obtained water from the old Burgess Springs, or Kokernot Spring at Kokernot Lodge. This spring can be traced back to 1684." The property was acquired by Daniel O. Murphy and when the Southern Pacific tracks reached what's now Alpine in 1882, the railroad bought the rights to Burgess Springs under a ninety-nine-year lease from Murphy, and the town known then as Osborne was renamed Murphyville. Herbert Kokernot recalled his father told him that a pump on the Burgess water hole was operated by a wood-burning boiler. A pipeline carried water to railroad tracks downtown. Later the railroad drilled wells along the tracks. The ninety-nine-year lease was dropped and the town became known as Alpine.

Alpine was only one of many Texas towns that grew up around the all-important water tanks, as railroads crisscrossed our state. A few of the many true "jerk-water" towns in Texas are:

Alma, in Ellis County, Benchley in Robertson County, Cypress in Harris County, Hockley in Harris County, Springfield in Jim Wells County, and Worthham in Freestone County. These railroad water tanks that spawned so many of Texas's "jerk-water" towns also made an impact on the culture of the people of Texas. The railroad water tanks were romanticized in a song written and sung about the Depression Era of the 1930s. "Waitin' For A Train" was made famous by early recording star Jimmie Rodgers, who was billed as the "Singing Brakeman," because of his experience working for the railroad. Nearly every man born during my generation knew the words to this mournful song of the times. Jimmie's recording went like this: "All around the water tank, waitin' for a train, I'm a thousand miles from home, sleepin' in the rain. Haven't got a nickel, not penny can I show. Get out, get out! you railroad bum, and he slammed the boxcar door." The railroad "bulls," or detectives, showed little mercy about kicking off those 1930s hobos, who knew they could catch a freight at any Texas water tank.

TYING THE KNOT TWENTY-FOUR HOURS A DAY

In the 1940s, Rockwall, Texas, county seat of Rockwall County, was known as the "Marriage Capital of Texas." The *Handbook of Texas*, considered the bible of Texas history, refers to Rockwall as "a marriage mecca, because of the ease with which a marriage license can be issued there." Many couples, some of which enjoyed only hours-long engagements, went to Rockwall to be married because a marriage license could be issued and the couple could be married without a waiting period. At least one Justice of the Peace had a neon-lighted sign in his yard, advertising his "24-hour availability to perform marriages." Rockwall County Commissioner Jerry Wimpee told this author that "this reputation as an easy place to get married may have existed as far back as the 1930s." He said that it was this city's image as a marriage mill that prompted his father, the elected County Clerk, and County Judge, to stop the procedures for issuing marriage licenses, as he felt it had developed into an industry that was not in the city's best interest!

REINHARDT, A TOWN THAT WAS LOST IN THE SHUFFLE

One of the bonuses we receive when we write about local trivia is the wealth of information that seems to ooze out of the woodwork as a result of the jogging of the collective memories of our readership. This was particularly true after we wrote a series of columns for a weekly Dallas-area newspaper, entitled "Lost in the Shuffle." It took several columns to give space to all the little towns that were once suburbs of Dallas, but which have vanished from the map as a result of being absorbed by Dallas as a part of its accelerated expansion. One of the forgotten small towns captured my interest because our old standby, the *Handbook of Texas*, pointed out that this late-nineteenth-century town in eastern Dallas County became a station on the Gulf, Colorado, and Santa Fe Railroad, and served chiefly as an overnight stop for fishing parties on White Rock Lake. Having grown up in old East Dallas and having spent much leisure time on the referred-to lake, I recalled seeing several businesses on Garland Road bearing the name "Reinhardt," but—having little interest in history—didn't attach much significance to the region at the time. I particularly remember there was a Reinhardt Baptist Church and a Reinhardt school. Our typical youthful lack of interest prevented us from exploring the area, which would have revealed the remains of a bygone era in Dallas County's history.

Established in 1886, Reinhardt had two stores and a population of 100. In conversation with a longtime resident of Reinhardt, and grandson of R. W. Euckert, the town's first postmaster, who built and operated a general merchandise store, I learned that the brick building that was built in 1903, and which housed Mr. Euckert's store, the post office, and his bank, still stands. The brick building replaced an original frame structure. Mr. Roy Ivey of Ivey's Building Materials on Peavy Road leases the brick building. He permitted us to photograph the original bank vault, which is still in the building. An interesting reference to the town of Reinhardt was found in the biography of "Daddy" Buckner, founder of Buckner's Orphan's Home. The book *Homeward Bound* tells us that "Due to a fire which burned the structure where church services were held at the Home's campus, the Home's church began meeting at the Baptist Church at Dawning Light, about three miles north of the Home at Reinhardt." The Reinhardt Elementary School, located at 10122 Losa Drive, and which is a part of the Dallas Independent School District, is not the original Reinhardt school. According to Mike Motley, the original Reinhardt school was a one- or two-room school located a short distance from the DISD school. The Santa Fe Railroad tracks that in days gone by served Reinhardt still exist, and they parallel Garland Road. They cross Peavy Road about two blocks east of Garland Road. The old Santa Fe depot, according to an old-time resident, was on what is now East Zacha, between Stephens and Fuller. Reinhardt was annexed into the City of Dallas on May 16, 1945. At that time, Reinhardt included a grand total of two square miles, according to the Dallas City Planning and Development Department. Reinhardt, like numerous other neighboring Dallas suburbs, was simply "Lost in the Shuffle."

DID YOU EVER WONDER WHY ANYONE WOULD NAME A TOWN "LICK SKILLET"?

According to the *History of Grayson County, Texas*, the Grayson County town of Pilot Grove, so named because "early travelers used this grove of pecan trees to steer their course," was once known as "Lick Skillet" because the stage stop had such good food the passengers licked their skillet clean.

KBOH, DALLAS'S FORGOTTEN RADIO STATION

In Karen Bullock's biography of "Father" R. C. Buckner, *Homeward Bound*, Dr. Bullock, in writing about the orphan's home founded by "Father" Buckner, writes, "On campus, another venture for the Home was established in the year, 1948. The Federal Communications Commission had granted a license for Buckner's Orphan's Home on May twelfth to operate and construct a 'Class B' frequency Modulation (FM) radio station on frequency 107.9

channel 300, its call letters, KBOH. The executive Board of the Baptist General Convention applied for and received permission to erect a tower on the Association's campgrounds near Cedar Hill. The Convention's radio department commenced broadcasting from three studios: the studio atop the Baptist Building headquarters at Pacific and Ervay Streets in Dallas; a branch studio on the campus of the Baptist Theological Seminary in Fort Worth; and a branch studio on the campus of Buckner's Orphan's Home."

STATE SONG MODIFIED

Most Texans know that our official state song is "Texas Our Texas." In 1959 something happened that necessitated modifying the lyrics of our state song from "Largest and grandest" to "boldest and grandest." This modification was made necessary when Alaska was given statehood. "At least," lamented one proud Texan, "we can brag that Texas is the largest, unfrozen state in the union!" A good sense of humor always helps.

MESQUITE'S EASTFIELD COLLEGE HAS A CEMETERY ON CAMPUS!

Colleges are bastions of learning. Usually it is the liberal arts that young men and women who grace the halls of Texas's schools of higher learning pursue. But one Dallas County college, by the very location of its beautiful campus, provides a course that vividly and poignantly goes beyond the usual academics in the school's official curriculum. I choose to call it "Cemetery 101." Some might choose to lump this course under the catch-all category of "The Humanities." I find it simply a powerful lesson in family history and compassion. The course costs nothing, requires no registration or books, and demands only a small amount of the student's time.

Wendy Flanagan, writing in the October 8, 1984 edition of the *Eastfield Era*, the school's newspaper, writes, "No more than 200 feet from the school's main entrance, students walk past a monument to one of Dallas County's early pioneers." Ms. Flanagan describes the monument this way: "Little remains of the legacy founded by Zachariah Motley except a small withered cemetery on the grounds of Eastfield College." Those buried in the little cemetery are the descendants of Zachariah and Mary Motley, who moved to Mesquite from Kentucky in 1856, settling on the Crittenden Survey three miles north of the Dallas County town of Scyene. In addition to the descendants buried in the small cemetery is the arm of one of Zachariah Motley's grandsons, and the foot of another. What was the Motley land is today the campus of Eastfield College. Zack Motley purchased some 6,000 acres of Dallas County, some at 25 cents an acre. On the land the two-and-a-half-story Motley mansion was erected; the cemetery was laid out nearby. The Motley land, according to Ms. Flanagan, "ran from the eastern banks of White Rock Lake to Bois d'Arc Island on the Trinity River."

One of the cemetery's major lessons of compassion was written about by Valerie Barna in the September 2, 1988 edition of the *Mesquite News*. "History is alive and still unfolding for students at Eastfield College, thanks to a small family cemetery 200 feet from the school's front door. The Motleys are buried there. They are descendants of Texas pioneers, Zachariah and Mary Motley. Also interred are slaves who served the Motleys during the brutal Civil War era. No one knows how many of the family servants rest within the confines of the fenced, quarter-acre plot. And 'Their names are known only to God,' said Joe Bailey Motley of Garland, great grandson of the family patriarch. In a family effort to restore the cemetery which had gotten in bad shape, said Joe Bailey Motley, the fence was taken down, repaired, and reinstalled. Motley moved the fence about forty feet to include the slave graves, and marked the area with a bronze plate he made himself. The plate reads, 'Known only to God.' This effort by Joe Bailey Motley reflects the continuation of the compassion the Motleys had for their slaves. This simple act to include the slaves in the family burial ground and afford them some recognition is the type of compassion one would expect from a family who saw the need to bury an arm and a foot amputated as the result of accidents suffered by family members. These dismembered body parts have markers. Joe Bailey Motley also made a bronze casting to mark the place where the right arm of his father, John Stephen Motley, was buried in 1894. The rest of John S. Motley is buried in Grand Prairie where he spent most of this life. John Motley died in 1925 at age 48. A marble stone marks the final resting place of the foot of another grandson of Zachariah Motley. Grover Cleveland Motley, 'Cleve,' as he was known, had his foot amputated after it was caught in the stirrup of a run-away horse. The foot was badly mangled and developed gangrene, which made amputation necessary. The marker over the unfortunate foot, reads, 'The foot of G. C. Motley buried June 5, 1911.' 'Cleve' Motley is buried in Dallas' Grove Hill Cemetery. I must admit I questioned why these body parts were interred in the cemetery, and in the interview with Joe Bailey Motley, he provided a straightforward answer that further illustrated the family's human compassion. Mr. Motley explained that at age 17, his father was working at the cotton gin in Reinhardt, Texas (a small town located near today's Garland Road and Buckner Blvd.), when his arm got caught in gin machinery. The young man was taken across the street to the Heart house, (the Hearts operated the gin). His arm was severed and held to his body only by sinew. A doctor was called out from Dallas and amputated the young man's arm. 'But why bury the body part in the cemetery?' I asked. 'They just couldn't throw it out for the birds to peck, and they couldn't burn it. We had the cemetery right near the house, it was just logical to bury the arm in the cemetery.' 'As a matter of fact,' Mr. Motley added, 'it had to be buried twice.' John said it felt like ants were stinging his arm. The arm was disinterred and sure enough, it was covered with ants. Then the arm was buried in an airtight box. I remember it well, it was a box my dad kept in his blacksmith shop." We are grateful to Valerie Barna and the *Mesquite News* and Wendy Flanagan and the *Eastfield Era* for permitting us to use excerpts from their stories about the Motley Cemetery.

"42," THE NATIONAL GAME OF TEXAS

The domino game "42" is said to be the "National Game of Texas," because it is so widely played across the Lone Star State, especially in rural Texas. It is said to have been invented in the spring of

1887 in the hamlet of Trappe Springs, now called Garner, located between Mineral Wells and Weatherford in Parker County. Legend has it that two boys were caught playing cards in the hayloft of a barn and were severely punished, as playing cards was considered a sin in the Bible Belt country. Because most families had a set of dominos in the home, the boys decided to try to create a game using playing card principles, but played with the acceptable dominos. The boys worked out the playing card game, which they found could be played with dominos. The boys taught the game to their strict parents. Seeing how much fun it was, the parents taught the game to their neighbors. The game became a favorite in the community because it could be played as a substitute for the forbidden deck of playing cards.

42 is not found in most other states except those bordering Texas, which were introduced to the domino game by migrating Texans. Incidentally, the dominos with which 42 is played are manufactured only in one place in the United States, and that is Waco, Texas. Puremco, Inc., which boasts of being the only domino manufacturer in America, began making the playing tiles in 1953. It sells about 100,000 sets each year, with 90 percent being sold in Texas. The game of 42 has gained a flock of new ambassadors in recent decades, and I mean a "flock" quite literally. "Winter Texans," or "snowbirds," as they are fondly called, migrate south into the warmer climate of Texas to avoid the cold of their northern and eastern winters. While making friends in Texas RV parks and state parks, they learn to play 42 from the locals. Upon return to their homes they "infect" their eastern and northern neighbors with this very addictive domino game. "This," said Puremco representatives, "has opened a brand new market for dominos."

YOU DON'T NEED A LICENSE TO GO SNIPE HUNTING IN TEXAS!

Most rural young people in Texas, especially boys, have taken their city cousins, and other greenhorns, on a snipe hunt, although the event will probably never be admitted to by the hunter! A snipe hunt is a traditional form of hazing of those folks not raised in a rural setting. The snipe hunt goes something like this: The city slicker is baited during the day by being told what he is missing by living in the city: "One thing he sacrifices is the thrill of hunting the wild game not found in suburbia, particularly the elusive and cunning creature known as the snipe that occupies the deep, dark woods surrounding the host's home. Much sought after and prized as a trophy, catching the elusive snipe, which only comes out in the dark of night, brings the hunter instant notoriety, and much praise! But catching the creature requires patience, nerves of steel, and lightening-fast reflexes. Especially the reflexes!"

After asking the visitor if he feels up to the challenge of snipe hunting, detailed instructions are given to the hunter, who is, in fact, the unwitting butt of the "hayseed's" cruel hoax. "Patience is the key to a successful hunt." After being instructed, the hunter is given a burlap bag, or tow sack; a two-foot length of cotton string, or small rope; a dish pan, or gallon bucket; and a tool with which to beat the bucket. The hunter is then led into the nearby woods or pasture at dark. Upon arrival at a predetermined spot deep within the woods, the hunter is given final instructions to ensure successfully catching the wary and very fleet of foot snipe: "Beat steadily on the bucket or pan for about five minutes, which will generally attract the elusive snipe," and which will give the perpetrators of the hoax ample time to slip silently away, leaving the victim "holding the bag," which may very well be the origin of that expression. "Then lay the pan, or bucket, on the ground, freeing both hands to tightly hold the sack. Hold the burlap bag open about waist high, gripping the rope or string tightly in one hand, making sure it isn't dropped. A snipe, attracted by the beating on the pan, will jump into the open sack. When the hunter feels the weight of the snipe in the bag, he must quickly (and speed is emphasized) wrap the string, or rope, snugly around the top of the sack, tying a tight knot to prevent the creature from wriggling from the sack." When the snipe is securely contained in the burlap bag, the hunter should bring it to the house. The hosts normally allow the "hunter" two to two and one-half hours in the velvet black woods, lighted only by the pale moonlight and the eerie green glow of lightning bugs, before they return to check the hunter's success at catching the mythical snipe that exists only in the minds of mischievous rural boys creating fun at the expense of their city cousins, who return to town somewhat embarrassed at being taken in, but with a healthy appreciation for those who live without electricity!

"Snipe hunting" is as old as the oldest Texan, but snipes are not the only mythical creatures to find a niche in the Texas mystique! Gene Fowler, a prolific chronicler of the life and legends of the land we call Texas, introduced us to a few of these in his entertaining story, "Crazy Critters," in the June 2001 issue of *Texas Highways* magazine. He told how many Texas tourists (especially first-timers) returned home with a picture postcard depicting Texas's best-known mythical critter, the "Jackalope." This antler-bearing jackrabbit still can be found thumping along the Texas prairie on postcards in souvenir shops from Amarillo to Brownsville. A creation of a taxidermist's fertile imagination, the jackalope has raised many an eyebrow since it first appeared on the Texas scene in 1934. Not quite so well known, but equally grotesque, is Waco's Orthlock, which Mr. Fowler tells us is a "mythical marsupial that basks on the banks of the Brazos River in Waco." The critter, says Fowler, "represents diversity, having fur, a duck bill, webbed back feet, a raccoon tail, antlers and wings." No doubt, this is another creation of a taxidermist whose talent went awry!

Each of these mythical Texas critters, with the exception of the snipe, who is so elusive that it has avoided capture by its many hunters, and therefore has never been seen, fall into the same category as Germany's wolpertingers, which we have seen on our visits to that country. One can hardly refer to these Texas mythical creatures as ridiculous, when ancient Greek mythology included such animals as the centaur (half man–half horse), and stories abound about the unicorn (a horselike animal with one horn in the middle of its head). One of the oldest Texas riddles is "What is the difference between a 'critter' and a 'varmint'?" The crude, but graphic answer is this: "A critter is what you see smushed on the side of a Texas roadway, and varmint is what you do after you see it!"

DID YOU EVER WONDER IF IT IS LEGAL TO PICK OUR STATE FLOWER?

Contrary to popular belief, there is no law against picking our state flower; however, there are laws against damaging roadside rights-of-ways. Picking wildflowers along our roadside rights-of-ways is discouraged by the Department of Transportation, as the plants need to reseed to come back next year for everyone to enjoy! If you do pick a bluebonnet, there is one surprise awaiting you. If you gently pull back one of the individual bonnets, you'll find a perfect cat's claw lurking inside!

THE LEGEND OF BUG TUSSLE, TEXAS

Just like the former Grayson County town of Toad Suck, and the barely believable communities of Cut and Shoot and Frognot, there was once a busy—not bustling but busy—town called Bug Tussle. I say "once busy," because, according to the *Handbook of Texas*, "It was once fashionable for couples to be married in Bug Tussle just so they could announce that they were married in Bug Tussle, Texas." Back in the 1950s, said one newspaper, Bug Tussle was a mecca for the curious as well as the altar-bound. As a legally elected justice of the peace, the late judge, James Bates Fink, who was also proprietor of the Bug Tussle Grocery store and filling station, officiated at far more weddings at his general store than he did fillups at his now weed-enshrouded gas pumps. Bug Tussle got so prosperous as a result of Judge Fink's marrying folks from all over the Southwest, it has been said, that a second store and filling station was opened up across the highway. Bug Tussle, incidentally, is located at the junction of Farm Road 1550 and State Highway 34, just north of Ladonia in Fannin County.

In a recent interview with ninety-year-old Robert Wishard, who was born in the Bug Tussle community and who married Judge Fink's daughter, and his Roxton, Texas banker son, Joe Wishard, both agreed that while the merchant J. P. did perform weddings, there were not as many as publicized. It seems old

This is an original photo of Judge James Bates Fink's general store in Bug Tussle. This store served as courtroom and marriage chapel for couples married by the justice of the peace. Photo provided by Joe Wishard, a former resident of Bug Tussle.

Ninety-year-old Robert Wishard (left) was born in Bug Tussle, Texas and married Judge Fink's daughter. He, along with his son, Joe Wishard, and Sandra Johnson (center) of nearby Honey Grove, Texas shared many Bug Tussle stories with the author (right) during a recent visit to his office. Photo courtesy of Sandra Johnson.

Judge Fink had a little help in spreading his notoriety from former *Dallas Morning News* columnist Frank X. Tolbert. Tolbert, one of Texas's most prolific chronicler of the tales of Texas's highways and byways, once quoted Judge Fink as saying he "offered Texas' cheapest weddings. For two dollars I would marry any couple, and for 50 cents extra, one of the loafers in the store would play, 'Here comes the bride' on a mouth organ during the ceremony."

But Judge Fink was not Bug Tussle's only well-known citizen, it seems. Dallas television weatherman–turned U.S. Congressman Dale Milford was born just two miles east of the store and claimed Bug Tussle as his birthplace. Although Bug Tussle was centered around Fink's grocery store and filling station, there was a blacksmith shop near the store. But the tiny town was not limited to these two enterprises! Robert Wishard told us how he remembered going with his father to the cotton gin as a boy. The gin, he said, was operated with steam engines. My friend, Nona Epps, who was born in the Bug Tussle suburb of Dial, spoke of the Bug Tussle gin in reverent tones, advising me that on Sunday, July 24, 1921 her sister, Elva Mann, was baptized in the water tank at the Bug Tussle cotton gin. Most gins, I learned, had a pond, or "tank," as stockmen call them, to provide water for the steam engines that powered the gin. Elva attended the Oak Ridge Church of Christ and the gin pond was probably the deepest body of water available for an immersion. Nona speculated that numerous area folks were baptized at the Bug Tussle cotton gin. When I first heard of the cotton-gin baptizing, as a city-bred fellow, I found it refreshingly amusing, somewhat like a scene from a Grandma Moses primitive painting. But in talking with several neighbors with a rural background, I learned the practice was quite common.

Like most towns with comical monikers, there are several stories as to how Bug Tussle got its name. "There are," said Joe Morrow, the former editor of the *Ladonia News*, "as many stories as there are people in the town." The *Handbook of Texas* says the town "was originally called Truss, after John Truss, who settled there." The most accepted version of the naming of Bug Tussle says that "Two old-time residents who wanted to change the name of the town, were engaged in a discussion of a proposed name when their attention was diverted by two tumblebugs (dung beetles), which were fighting on the ground. 'Look at those bugs tussle,' one was reported to have remarked." Almost as though the men took the nature show as an omen, the argument was settled and the town was christened. The town was founded in the 1890s and had a post office in 1893–1894. Bug Tussle reported only six residents by 1962. A brief revitalization of the town with the curious name brought the population to fifteen in 1990. The town's city limits sign on the highway has been stolen a reported seventy times. Judge Fink's dilapidated general store and service station, or, if one is romantically inclined, "marriage chapel" is today a weed-shrouded, boarded-up hull of its former self.

Mark Hill of Mount Pleasant, Texas wrote a Dallas newspaper columnist a letter that gives some insight into life in Bug Tussle in its heyday! Mr. Hill writes, "My grandfather was Judge James Bates Fink, who once owned the store there in Bug Tussle. He was justice of the peace for years. The column brought back many childhood memories, of sitting in the store, watching my grandfather hold J. P. sessions. Spit cans were all around the stove for the farmers." Yes! Bug Tussle really gave up a lot when it gradually faded into oblivion, except for its comical moniker!

One thing that hasn't been lost in the Bug Tussle community is its sense of humor! Joe T. Morrow, editor and publisher of the neighboring *Honey Grove Signal-Citizen*, and the *Ladonia News*, printed up windshield stickers honoring Bug Tussle's imaginary football team, the "BUG TUSSLE TUSSLERS." Morrow explained that the stickers, like some of the tales about the community, were purely the result of an agile imagination. "After all," Morrow continued, "if a community with a population of seven were to get together an eleven person team, it would have to employ some outside players." Editor Morrow's "booster stickers," it seems, made Bug Tussle the only town in Texas having football boosters with no team to boost! Seems like a turn of events that would give the loafers who once hung out at Judge Fink's store enough talking material for a month! Loafers, it appears, were an integral part of the makeup of Judge Fink's establishment. They were significant enough to warrant Frank Tolbert to write, in one of his columns, "It happens that I knew the late Judge Fink, when he was lord of the hamlet! In those gala years one of the distinguished loafers was said to be a champion spitter of tobacco." Mr. Tolbert did not elaborate on whether the championship involved distance, quantity, or how adroit the spitter was at hitting the well-placed tomato cans. Regardless, our opinion is that a lively discussion about the prospects of a winning season for the imaginary Bug Tussle Tusslers, especially against such local teams as the Mud-Dig Maulers from nearby Mud-Dig, or the neighboring Oak Ridge squirrels, would not only be more lively, but much more sanitary than the daily tobacco spitting competition!

ANSWERING "HAVE YOU EVER WONDERED" QUESTIONS

I think the most enjoyment one can experience from collecting Texas trivia, aside from improving our own knowledge about the Lone Star State, is the answering of a question posed by a fellow Texan who has pondered a particular facet of Texana. And there are more than enough of these to go around! It gives a particular sense of satisfaction to see the look of amazement on their faces when they receive a particularly surprising answer. We have assembled a selection of topics that our readers have, from time to time, asked about. Perhaps your face will register the same look of surprise we have seen so many times before.

WHEN WAS THE LAST HOSTILE INDIAN ATTACK ON WHITES IN TEXAS? The last Indian attack on whites occurred in 1874 at Adobe Walls, Hutcheson County. The raid was led by Comanche Chief Quanah Parker, who assembled a war party and attacked this buffalo camp, instigated by a warmongering medicine man. Chief Parker, the last Comanche Indian chief, was the son of an Indian father and a white mother, Cynthia Ann Parker, who was captured as a small girl at Fort Parker, Texas. Some contend that the last action with Indians in Texas was after 1874 when General Ranald S. Mackenzie defeated a large force of Indians at the Palo Duro Canyon, one of the Indians' last strongholds in Texas, making it safe for Anglos to make a permanent settlement in that area.

JUNETEENTH: HOW DID THIS TEXAS HOLIDAY FOR BLACKS GET ITS NAME? June 19th is the date in 1865 that Union general Granger for the first time announced the emancipation of Texas's slaves. The announcement was made in Galveston. Texas Negroes simply shortened nineteenth to "teenth."

WHAT WAS THE ORIGIN OF TEXAS'S LONE STAR FLAG? Johanna Troutman is given official credit for designing the "Lone Star" flag of Texas, although there were several flags bearing the lone star used in various Texas battles. Mrs. Troutman is referred to in the *Handbook of Texas* as "The Betsy Ross of Texas."

WHAT IS THE MEANING OF THE COLORS IN THE TEXAS FLAG? The colors in the flag do have a special meaning: red—courage, white—liberty, and blue—loyalty.

WHEN WAS THE LAST OFFICIAL PUBLIC HANGING? The last official hanging in Texas took place on July 30, 1923 in Waco when Roy Mitchell was executed for eight murders he committed during a reign of terror.

WHAT WERE THE NAMES OF THE FAMOUS CATTLE TRAILS IN TEXAS? In the 1800s, Texas ranchers used four major cattle trails to drive their cattle to railheads so they could be shipped to market. They were: (1) The Shawnee Trail, (2) The Chisholm Trail, (3) The Western Trail, and (4) The Goodnight-Loving Trail.

HOW LONG IS A YARD IN TEXAS? This question was more important to early Texas colonists than you may think. It was certainly more important to the women who bought fabric for sewing. According to the *Southwestern Historical Quarterly*, while Texas was under Spanish rule, the measurement of a yard was the Mexican yard, which was thirty-three inches. It was not until 1832 that merchantmen introduced the English yard, which was thirty-six inches.

WHERE WAS TEXAS'S WATERLOO? For nearly 200 years the name Waterloo has been synonymous with defeat and doom! *Webster's New World Dictionary* defines Waterloo as follows: "town in Belgium, scene of Napoleon's final defeat. (1815) any disastrous or decisive defeat." Was it a foretaste of things to come, or just a coincidence that our state capital, Austin, was originally named Waterloo? According to the 1992–93 *Texas Almanac*, in 1839 the Texas Congress authorized a commission to select a permanent capital. It was to be north of the Old San Antonio Road between the Trinity and Colorado Rivers. It was to lie on major north-south and east-west trade routes, and near the center of the state. The commission selected a site near Waterloo, an outpost on the Colorado River, about 80 miles northeast of San Antonio. In building the city, town lots were sold in 1839 at a total income of $182,585, which practically paid for the government buildings under construction.

HOW MANY KINDS OF CACTUS ARE THERE IN TEXAS? A sticky subject to touch on is Texas's cacti. The Texas cactus is found no other place in the world than the Western Hemisphere. Because of Texas's extensive area and climatic conditions favorable to the growth of cacti, the state contains over 100 species, representing the widest assortment of cacti found in any state in the United States. The species range from the widespread prickly pear to a rarer variety found only in El Paso County. Texas also grows cacti of radically different sizes. One may find the "button cactus," which is no larger than a dime, as well as the "barrel cactus," also known as the "fishhook cactus," which may grow to half a ton. As formidable as their protective spines may seem, they are, with proper preparation, edible for men and cattle. Texas cacti have a wide variety of interesting and descriptive names. Some of their names are: hunger, starvation, flapjack, dumpling, strawberry, prickly pear, blind pear, cow's tongue, night blooming cactus, devil's head, horse-killer cactus, and the "Glory-of-Texas" cactus, which, incidentally, grows mainly in Mexico. This is our story on cactus, and you are stuck with it!

WHY IS BEAUMONT SUCH A MISNOMER? Among those Texas cities having an unsuitable name, one has to include the beautiful city of Beaumont, which was founded in 1835 when its first reputed Anglo settler, Noah Tevis, sold fifty acres of land to the Thomas Huling Company through its agent, Henry Millard. A townsite was laid out and named Beaumont, which in French means "beautiful mountain." Some say it was named for a slight elevation southeast of the city. Others say he named it for a relative. Beaumont seems to be a preposterous name, since its highest elevation is only thirty-six feet above sea level!

DID YOU EVER WONDER WHY TEXAS CONVICTS CAN BLAME THE CIVIL WAR FOR THEIR PLACE OF CONFINEMENT? Although they may not know it, or even care, many convicted felons in Texas can blame the Civil War if they aren't happy with their state-assigned "home away from home"! The *Handbook of Texas* tells us that agriculture was the foundation of the early economy of Brazoria County. Sugar and cotton plantations along the Brazoria River and the deeper creeks flourished during the antebellum period in Texas, making Brazoria the wealthiest county in Texas. It was a typically Southern society based on slavery. That civilization was destroyed by the Civil War. Agricultural production declined sharply with the freeing of the slaves. While many plantations were broken into small farms and turned into pasture lands, other plantations became Ramsey, Clemens, and Darrington, prison farms of the Texas Department of Corrections. Now, agricultural efforts on this land still exist, but they are being performed not under the watchful eye of the master's overseer, but under the eye of an armed guard whose job it is to help the laborer learn that "Crime doesn't pay!"

OTHER THAN CHILI COOK-OFFS, WHAT IS TERLINGUA KNOWN FOR? One of Texas's natural resource locations has been overshadowed by modern events. The "ghost town" of Terlingua has made a name for itself as the "chili cook-off capital of the world." This newly found "resource" has almost brought this once-bustling mining town back into the classification of "living." The town was established as a silver mine; however, it did not develop into a community until a large deposit of "quicksilver," or mercury, was discovered and profitably mined. After the mining stopped, the town vanished!

Chapter Four

TRUTH IS STRANGER THAN FICTION

Texans, who are famous for "tall tales," are frequently accused of exaggerating when the story they are telling is so bizarre that it sounds like the product of an overactive imagination, when actually the story is 100 percent true. In these cases we are prone to say "Truth is stranger than fiction!" Some of the legends and folklore of the Lone Star State are candidates for suspicion in the eyes of the state's "Doubting Thomases." We have devoted an entire section of this book to prime examples of unbelievable, but very true, Texas legends, which we believe will be told and re-told by even the most skeptical of readers. We have made every effort to research their veracity. It is our hope that these bits of legend and lore will prove that most anything is possible in Texas!

BURIED TREASURES: YOURS FOR THE FINDING!

Of all the legends that go to make up Texas's exciting history, none is better known, nor has stirred more excitement in the past, especially in the royal court of Spain, than early Spanish explorers' reports of the discovery of "seven cities of gold" in what then was North Texas. In the year 1540 the legend was to result in Spanish explorer Coronado's futile expedition in search of these treasures, which were supposedly rich beyond all imagination. To Texas history buffs today, this disappointing expedition was eons ago. But Texas holds many more legends of undiscovered buried treasures of more recent vintage, which we, like Coronado of old, can explore through the pages of this book of Texas legend and lore. We hope you will feel enriched by their revelation, in your mind, if not in your pocket.

SEWING MACHINE WEALTH ON PADRE ISLAND How many of you remember your mother's or grandmother's old Singer treadle sewing machine? It may have had a connection to a Texas buried treasure. According to the *Handbook of Texas*, Padre Island may be hiding a personal fortune. The island was occupied in 1800 by Padre Nicholas Balli, who was granted the island by the Spanish crown. It was from him that the island got its name. Although it was plagued by ownership disputes over the years, the Balli family occupied the island until the last of the Balli family moved out in 1844. It was apparently deserted until 1847, when John V. Singer, master of the *Alice Sadell*, was wrecked there. Singer built a home on Balli's old Rancho Cruz, and established the Las Cruces Ranch. He also bought and sold land on the island without securing proper titles. Before the Civil War John V. Singer acquired a large fortune from his share of his brother's sewing machine company. A Unionist, he was reputed to have buried a large treasure of coins and jewelry before he left Texas. There is no record of anyone finding such a treasure as this. Perhaps "fun in the sun" is not the only reason you should make Padre Island a place to vacation?

SALADO TREASURE CHAMBER A yellowing clipping from a now defunct Dallas newspaper dated February 1965 and bearing the dateline "Salado, Texas" indicates that "Only a few feet of crumbling limestone needed to be pierced before two Dallasites would become billionaires." This reference was to the pair's search for a room in a long-sealed cave near this Central Texas town, probably best known for the eatery "The Stagecoach Inn." The room, according to one of the diggers, is filled with enough treasure to give them their own "Ft. Knox." The man, who alleges that he had been in the room before a rockslide covered its entrance, depicts the room as containing "2,000 bars of gold, 600 bars of silver and two stacks of coins and artifacts." He said he got lost in the labyrinth, became tired and hungry, and feared for his life. "He ignored the treasure—even a life-size golden bull's head with ruby eyes, and got out of the caves." After being hospitalized he returned and discovered that a rockslide had buried the entrance to the treasure. Nothing in this timeworn report indicated that the hunters or anyone else ever found the fortune. It would appear today that the gold jackpot is still there for the finding!

SPANISH TREASURE IN THE BIG THICKET? It was Texas's Big Thicket's role in the Civil War that I was researching when I came upon a trivia nugget about the possibility of Spanish buried treasure in the already intrigue-filled Big Thicket of East Texas. This finding came from an October 1931 edition of the *Beaumont Enterprise*. Writing in this East Texas paper, Dean Tevis laid out a tale fit to start the "Lust for gold" juices coursing through the veins of treasure hunters everywhere. He describes how, with help from a few locals, help which, contrary to most other areas of Texas, might be hard to come by here due to the clannishness of "Thicket" folks, you might find a trail into the Thicket once known as "The Village Mills-Saratoga Highway." The writer says that "It was highway, at least of sorts." Earlier it had been an Indian trail; the Alabamas knew about it. "The great beech trees have queer dimmed marks made by strange hatchets, beneath which money hunters have dug holes in the woods floor." There are beliefs that beneath each of the carvings lie gold treasure of some sort, but one is a mite doubtful that the traveling Spaniards, usually afoot, could carry enough gold to favor all the trees that are marked. Some of the local Indians say that they heard the stories passed on by their grandparents. Far be it for me to rush into the already mysterious Big Thicket to satisfy my gold fever on such tenuous evidence.

CHEWING GUM INTRODUCED TO U.S. BY SANTA ANNA

Charles Panati's book *Origins of Everyday Things* surprises us with evidence that the Mexican general, who was defeated by the Texian army in 1836, which resulted in Texas achieving independence from Mexico, is responsible for one of America's favorite flavorful treats, chewing gum. The book relates the story this way: After Texas became a state in 1845, Santa Anna entered the United States and settled on Staten Island. He brought with him a large chunk of chicle (the dried milky sap or latex of the sapodilla tree that grows in Mexico). Chicle was known to the Aztecs as chicli. In 1869 he introduced the chicle to local photographer and inventor Thomas Adams, who failed in an attempt to convert the resin chemically into a synthetic rubber. Adams, noting how avidly Santa Anna and his son loved to chew the chicle, imported a large quantity of it. He decided to market it as an alternative to the then popular wads of paraffin wax sold to chew. Adams sold the small tasteless balls of chicle to a Hoboken drug store for a penny a piece. The product was labeled "Adam's New York gum." John Colgan, a pharmacist from Louisville, Kentucky, was the first person to add flavor to chicle in 1875. The chicle was marketed in long thin strips, notched so a druggist could break off a penny's worth. The product was marketed along the East Coast by Adam's son, who was a traveling salesman. The chicle was sold in several flavors.

SPOILS OF WAR CAN BE STRANGE: SANTA ANNA'S LEG CAPTURED IN MEXICAN-AMERICAN WAR

Based on a bizarre story written by Paul Wood in the *Champaign-Urbana (IL) News-Gazette*, the victims of the brutal Mexican General Santa Anna at the Alamo and Goliad were avenged by the Fourth Regiment, Illinois Volunteers in the Mexican-American War. These brave Illinoisans literally knocked the props from under the tyrannical "Napoleon of the West" in a most undignified way! By permission of the *Champaign-Urbana (IL) News-Gazette*, we are presenting the story verbatim as it appeared on March 30, 1998.

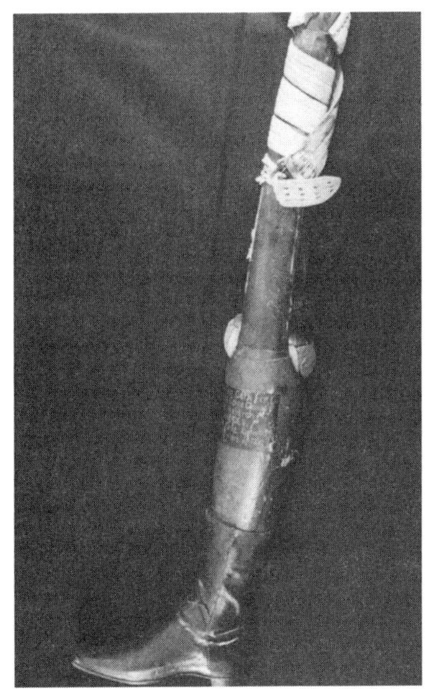

Santa Anna's artificial leg, captured by the Illinois Guard during the Mexican-American War. Photo used by permission of the Illinois State Military Museum.

"SANTA ANNA'S LEG TOOK A LONG WALK. CERRO GORDO—General Antonio Lopez de Santa Anna could be lucky in war, notably at the Alamo, but he had a problem with food. He lost his leg in the so-called French Pastry War, fought between Mexico and France in 1838. Then in 1847, facing the United States in the battle of Cerro Gordo, Mexico, he stopped paying attention to the war long enough to linger over a roast chicken. His lunch was interrupted by an uninvited regiment of Illinoisans, who ate the general's chicken and carried off his cork leg. Santa Anna hobbled away to fight another day. It was a huge victory for the 4th Regiment Illinois Volunteers, who also discovered a hoard of gold used to pay Mexican soldiers. It was an even bigger victory for Capt. Robert E. Lee, whose fame led, eventually, to his command of Confederate forces 15 years later in the Civil War. Some of the soldiers returned to Piatt County, where the town of Griswold was renamed Cerro Gordo in commemoration of the battle. The volunteers' regiment would eventually become the Illinois National Guard, and its trophy of war, Santa Anna's cork leg, now resides in the Guard's museum, Camp Lincoln in Springfield. Over the years, the Mexican government has asked for Santa Anna's leg back. Not that it would do the general any good, though it might show a little sensitivity. Artificial legs aren't as funny as they were in the 1850s, when veterans charged a nickel or a dime for curiosity-seekers to handle the leg in hotel bars. Santa Anna's prosthesis had 30 minutes of fame earlier this month, when the Fox animated television series, 'King of the Hill' did a show on the topic—a surprisingly accurate one. It tells how the general was surprised while eating chicken and credits the Ill. Volunteers. The show's one error had the leg traveling to Texas as a historical portable exhibit. Mark Whitlock of Camp Lincoln's Illinois State Military Museum says the leg is going nowhere, ever. 'It's an important part of Illinois history,' he said. Cerro Gordo's place in history is marked by an inscription on the shin of the leg: 'General Santa Anna's cork leg, captured at the battle of Cerro Gordo, Mexico, by Private A, Waldon, First Sergeant, Sam Rhoades, Second Sergeant John M. Gill April 18, 1847, all of the Fourth Regiment Illinois volunteers of the Mexican War.' There are still Rhoades and Gills in Piatt County, but no one contacted by the *News-Gazette* could remember a family history involving the war against Mexico, chicken dinners and a cork leg. Helping untangle the Cerro Gordian knot is Sheila Coffman, who now lives near LaPlace. She's heard stories of the victory and how a Central Illinois town got a Spanish name. It means Fat Hill. She pointed out that the name is also fitting because of the town's elevated status as one of the high points between St. Louis and Danville, she said."

We are grateful to the *Champaign-Urbana News-Gazette* for permitting us to share this bizarre story about the Mexican general who so brutalized the Texians in their fight for justice during the Texas Revolution.

TEXAS MULES BEAT STEAMER IN RACE, WINNING $100,000 WAGER

The much-publicized arrival of mail and passenger service by the Butterfield Overland stage was to create an excitement unrivaled in the period of 1846–1861. But perhaps rivaling the initial excitement was the $100,000 bet between John Butterfield of the famed stage line and Captain Harrison of the Great Eastern Steamer. For the details of this high-stakes transportation wager we take the details from *A History of Grayson County*, by Mattie D. Lucas and Mita H. Hall, published in 1936. "Harrison bet his steamer could go all the way around South America and beat the mules, (Butterfield's stage mules), into San Francisco: The stake $100,000.00. The great liner carried 7,000 yards of sail and her eight engines could turn out 11,000 horsepower. Three months preparation were given. Butterfield spent $50,000 in new equipment; new coaches were purchased and held in readiness at many points along the route, experienced drivers and only the fastest mules and horses were held in readiness at the change station. The starting time arrived with the whole nation watching. Around Cape Horn sailed the steamer and up the Pacific, with all sails spread. Over the prairie sped the Texas mules. In Sherman, as at every other station, the entire population watched for the first faint cloud of dust; a fresh driver and fresh teams were ready and before the wheels had ceased turning, traces were unfastened and in went the fresh team; if coaches were changed the driver threw the mail and away they dashed! Yells and cheers followed the rocking stage as long as a cloud of dust was visible. The mules seemed to realize they carried the honor of Texas and raced for all they were worth. The frontier had never known such excitement—side bets almost equaled those of the principal. Twenty days of wild driving and quick changes—Twenty days and the last relay dashed into San Francisco. The ovation was led by Butterfield himself. For it was thirty-six hours later before the Great Eastern docked—The Texas mules had won!" We gratefully acknowledge *A History of Grayson County* for this description of the Butterfield Mail's race against the clock.

STARTING A CEMETERY THE HARD WAY

The town of Van Horn, county seat of Culberson County in the Diablo Mountains of West Texas, is noted for its healthy, dry climate. During Van Horn's early days, Bill Goynes, a cattle rancher, made the decision to tout the town as a healthy place to settle. It is said he did so by hanging the following sign in the Clark Hotel: "VAN HORN IS SO HEALTHY WE HAD TO SHOOT A MAN TO START A CEMETERY." Ironically, afterwards Goynes got into an argument with his brother-in-law over a watering hole. Guns were drawn and shots fired. Goynes was killed and became the first person to be buried in the Van Horn cemetery.

THE LEGEND OF THE GHOSTS OF "THE SINGING RIVER"

Although I spent many delightful summer days and nights crabbing and fishing in the brackish waters of the San Bernard River in Brazoria County, as the guest of my friends, the Martins, I was never privileged to witness the wailing sounds of the legendary ghosts of that river. Looking back at those days in the 1960s and recalling the eerie sight of the hoary Spanish moss hanging, like a hag's hair, almost to the water from the gnarled boughs of the ancient oaks that lined the riverbanks, I am sure that if I dared to venture a little more downriver, especially in the still of the night when the river was lighted only by the shimmering moonlight and a few scattered pier lights, I would have encountered the ghosts of the San Bernard. It was not until much later that I learned that the San Bernard is known as "The Singing River." The reason for this title is spooky, to say the least. Many stories, each reminiscent of Halloween, are told about this South Texas river. Locals gladly relate these stories when asked about the mournful tones that can be heard on the river's lower reaches. The haunting melody that can be heard is explained in the following ways. One of the most fascinating has to do with the wail of a violin allegedly heard after 100 years. The mystery has never been solved. Some say a former pirate from Jean Lafitte's band played his violin along the riverbank after he was murdered. They insist his ghost still plays the plaintive music. Another South Texas legend has it that a longboat full of slaves overturned in the river's mouth. Chained in place, the slaves could not escape the chilly waters of the San Bernard, and some say what is heard are the final wails of the dying slaves.

Yet another legend tells of a young musician whose bride-to-be died just hours before the wedding. The grief-stricken lover played his violin nightly to console himself. Ever since his death, his sad song continues. Is the sad music just "escaping swamp gas," as some scientists would have us believe? What do scientists know about the legends that are a part of the Texas mystique?

CURSES!

The title of this piece is not meant as an oath of exasperation. One cannot write a complete book on the legends and lore of Texas without including some of the best-known, and often believed, instances where God, or the Gods, were called on to bring evil or injurious punishment to someone or to some entity. That is what is commonly known as a "curse." Whether you wish to believe the subsequent harm was a result of someone's supplication to the Gods, or merely a coincidence, is your choice. The following examples of "curses" recorded in state or local histories are believed by many, especially the superstitious, to be the result of intonations made by persons having supernatural powers. The fact that they have been kept alive by locals who are of the opinion that they are a part of their regional history makes them worthy of exposure in print. Whether real or a figments of overactive imaginations, these Texas curses are worth exploration.

THE CURSE OF CHIPITA RODRIQUEZ The story of Chipita Rodriquez, who was, says the *Handbook of Texas*, "The only woman legally hanged in Texas," is one mixed with fact and the legends of the Rio Grande Valley. Chipita is the diminutive of Chepa, the nickname for Josefa. She lived in a hut on the Welder ranch lands on the Aransas River. San Patricio court records show that in August of 1863, Chipita and Juan Silvera were indicted for murdering a man named John Savage, who was a horse trader. Savage was carrying gold into Mexico for purchasing. His body was found in the Aransas River near Chipita's hut. When the court met in San Patricio, then county seat of San Patricio County, Juan Silvera was convicted of second-degree murder and given a five-year prison sentence. Chipita was convicted of first-degree murder and Judge Benjamin Neal sentenced her to be hanged. Mercy was recommended because her conviction was based largely on circumstantial evidence, but Judge Neal ordered her to be hanged on November 13, 1863. She was hanged on a mesquite tree in the Nueces River bottom near San Patricio and her body was buried in an unmarked grave.

Legends abound about this hanging because there are so many stories about Chipita's innocence. It was later said that a dying man confessed to the murder. It was even said that Chipita's long-lost son committed the murders. One report was that the gold Savage carried was found, either before or just after the trial. Regardless of the facts, it was felt by local residents that Chipita's hanging was at least questionable! And her possible innocence is the reason her ghost haunts the riverbanks where she was hanged. Some have said the questionable hanging put a curse on San Patricio, bringing about its death, including losing its position as county seat to Sinton in 1893.

THE CURSE ON THE COURTHOUSE CLOCK It is said that one Texas town has a clock that is cursed. Albert Howard was hanged in Gonzalez, Texas in 1921. Howard died while protesting his innocence! While waiting to be hanged, he watched the clock on the Gonzalez County courthouse as it ticked away his final hours. He swore that his "innocence would be demonstrated by the clock, which would never keep correct time, again." Since his hanging in 1921, the four faces of the clock have never kept the same time, despite attempts to repair the clock. A conversation with sheriff's deputies in Gonzales confirmed the story about the clock with a curse, but we were advised that in recent years the clock has been repaired to show the correct time

THE CURSE IN THE HOTEL REGISTRY Although not on the coast, one Texas town was once a shipping port second only to Galveston! But that was before the curse written in the hotel register! The quaint, picturesque bed-and-breakfast town of Jefferson on East Texas's Caddo Lake was once known as "Riverport to the Southwest." This bustling shipping town would have presented great financial opportunities for railroad magnate Jay Gould's new railroad. The "Wizard of Wall Street" offered to build his railroad through Jefferson if the town would furnish the right-of-way. The city fathers voted not to furnish the right-of-way or subsidize Gould's railroad in any way. A livid Gould, unaccustomed to being shunned, appealed to the Gods to bring this arrogant town to its knees by writing his "curse" in the Excelsior Hotel's register upon checking out prior to his departure. The railroad tycoon wrote, "Grass will grow in your streets, and bats will roost in your vacant houses." His prediction was that without a railroad the town would decline. The curse was signed with a drawing of a bird—a Jaybird, no doubt! Subsequent events, which resulted in a change of waterways that made the town inaccessible to shipping, ensured the town's decline. On our first visit to this once-bustling riverport, we did indeed see grass growing in the middle of some streets. We had no time, nor inclination, to inspect the vacant homes of the town to search for bats!

THE ONLY SOUTHERN CITY TO FALL INTO THE HANDS OF A MOB OF WOMEN

One of the most unbelievable, yet true, bits of Texas folklore is the true story of how, during the Civil War, one Texas city fell into the hands of a mob of angry women. The story is recounted in *A History of Grayson County* by Mattie D. Lucas and Mita H. Hall. The setting is the Grayson County city of Sherman in the waning years of the Civil War. "The Southern Confederacy," write the narrators, "for the last two years of its existence, maintained in the county site [*sic*] of all organized counties, a commissary department, where was kept all kinds of foodstuffs which that particular county produced. This produce was raised by sort of a tithing process. From these commissaries rations could be drawn by passing soldiers and all 'war widows' were privileged to draw rations there. The number of 'war widows' was very large in Grayson County, and many of them needed the rations badly. The officer in charge of the Sherman commissary was Major Blaine, a veteran of the Texas war for Independence. By reason of bountiful crops, the Sherman commissary was unusually well supplied with grain, flour, and meat, and became well known to all the 'war widows' of the county. However, they became dissatisfied with the sameness of the rations they were permitted to draw. By this time trade between Texas and Mexico had developed into large proportions. Texas cotton was hauled to the Rio Grande and sold for a big price, and the money invested in such necessary supplies as people were deprived of by the blockade. The report started among 'war widows' of Grayson County that this trade was being carried on by the government, and that all these luxuries, among them tea and coffee had been purchased by the government for the use of, families of the soldiers, but that the officers in charge were selling them to the people and keeping he money. The 'war widows' of the county banded themselves together in a secret organization, determined to get what was coming to them. One day in the winter of 1864, the county seat found itself in the hands of a mob of wild-eyed, desperate and hungry women, armed with guns, axes, and sledgehammers and clubs. The mob numbered more than 125 and they came to town on horseback. The leader was a Mrs. Savage, and she was a born leader. Had she have been a man she would have been at least a general in the army. Who came to her obeyed her every command. The women surrounded the commissary, and Mrs. Savage, as spokesman, told Major Blain that she knew a soldier's ration included sugar, coffee, and tea, and that she knew he had been withholding these things from the rations of 'war widows' of Grayson County. She stated that she had come for what belonged to them, and would stand no foolishness. Major Blain gracefully surrendered. Producing the keys he escorted the ladies through his warehouse, showing them he had none of these things. The ladies were not satisfied and argued that what they sought was in some other building. Most of the business houses were locked and empty, but with hammers and axes, the women continued their search for the coveted luxuries. On the east side of the square was a general store kept by I. Heilbroner, a subject of Great Britain. He had quite a stock of goods brought to Sherman from Mexico. At the first sign of trouble he locked the doors and got out of the way. In due course of time the mob—and it was a wild mob by then, increased by a number of Sherman women—reached the store, broke down the doors and were helping themselves when Charles Quantrell* entered the store. He was alone and gave no orders, nor made any threats. He simply said in a low, well-modulated voice, 'What would your husbands think if they could see you? They are at the front, enduring all kinds of hardships, hungry, barefooted, doing their duty without complaint. What would they think of you?' He talked to them until they became ashamed, disbanded and left the goods, nailing up the doors of the store as they left. This was probably the only time Quantrell ever addressed a 'sewing circle,' and probably the only instance of an American town being in the hands of a mob of women."

We are grateful to the authors of *A History of Grayson County* for preserving this marvelous bit of Texas folklore. We are grateful to the family of Mita Hall for granting us permission to reprint this story from her fine book.

BUFFALOES PRESENT UNUSUAL THREAT TO EARLY TEXAS TELEGRAPH

According to the *History of Grayson County, Texas,* published in 1981, strange as it sounds, buffaloes presented a threat to construction of early telegraph lines in North Texas. The book tells the story this way: "A notable construction in Grayson County was the first telegraph lines, built by the War Department to connect to army posts on the Texas frontier, and to be used for private messages. The first pole was set in Denison, Texas November 12, 1874. Some 3,500 poles had been distributed along the proposed line to Fort Richardson." The story goes on to tell us that while some posts were lost to prairie fires, other posts were pushed over by buffaloes scratching their backs on the posts. These oversized "scratching posts" were no doubt irresistible to the shaggy-haired animals who made the Texas prairie their home.

---

* Charles Quantrell was the guerrilla chieftain of the South. In company with Jesse and Frank James he had formed a gang of outlaws that was infamous during the Civil War. In the spring of 1863 he had drifted into Grayson County, Texas.

SCION OF "WALL STREET WITCH" USED WOODEN LEG TO PROVE TEXAS RESIDENCE

When I attended a Christmas party in the new "Old Victorian" home of my friends, Howard and Linda Tygrett, in the picturesque town of Terrell, I got more than a stockingful of surprises. Howard, knowing my penchant for collecting unusual facts about Texas, was quick to point out that their recent move into what is known as the Jarvis-Rutledge house had opened the door to numerous facts that might fit snugly into my Texas trivia collection. Howard and Linda's house was built in 1887 for J. O. Terrell, lawyer, judge, and onetime candidate for governor of Texas. Mr. Terrell, I learned, was the stepson of R. A. Terrell, for whom the town was named. Although the Tygretts' old Victorian home was tastefully decorated, its history further enhanced it in my eyes. In addition to the history of Howard's house, I related to him the story of the first automobile trip in Texas, originating in Terrell, and made by the very wealthy Terrell resident, Ned Green. Howard's eyes lighted up at the mention of Mr. Green's name. I learned that this same Mr. Green had a bizarre connection with this very house.

Colonel E. H. R. (Ned) Green (1868–1936) was the only son of Hetty Green, known as "The Witch of Wall Street," and one of the wealthiest women in the world. Hetty Green had sent her son to Terrell in 1893 to run a railroad. Ned did, indeed, buy the first automobile in Terrell and Dallas, and had the first automobile accident in Texas. But that's another story. When Col. Green left Texas to run his mother's empire elsewhere, he wished to maintain his residence in Texas (partly for state income tax reasons). How Col. Green did this was most bizarre! He rented a room in what is now my friend, Howard Tygrett's, house from the Jarvis family, paying $25 a month for twenty years. Col. Green never set foot in the house, but stored one of his wooden legs and a pair of trousers in an armoire to establish residence. The armoire is now in the Terrell Heritage Museum. The Attorney General of Texas attempted to introduce the trousers into evidence in a trial before the United States District Court to obtain the inheritance tax on Col. Green's estate.

BIRTH OF A SAYING

Early Texas sayings were sometimes born out of comical circumstances. One such saying, it has been written, originated in a Sherman, Texas bar owned by George Stamps. During a big Fourth of July celebration in Sherman, Stamps ran out of nutmegs. The story is told that Stamps took some hickory nuts, filed them in the shape of nutmegs, and placed them in a saucer with a grater hanging nearby. This, is said, did all right with friends and neighbors, but one day a stranger called for a drink with nutmeg and a grater. When the stranger began to grate the faux nutmegs, Stamps is supposed to have said, "Look here, stranger, them nutmegs costs like hell," and took the hickory nut. The stranger drank his whiskey plain and left. "That costs like Stamps's nutmegs" was a saying around Sherman for many years, signifying something cost more than its worth.

DEATH FROM A TEXAS WILDFLOWER

The well-known cowboy ballad "I'm Back in the Saddle, Again" contains a phrase that for the longest time I couldn't make heads or tails of. The phrase went like this: "Where the longhorn cattle feed on the lowly Jimson weed." As I'm not a stockman or rancher the term "jimson weed" was unknown to me. I honestly thought the singer must be saying gypsum weed, referring to the soil in which the weed grew. This, I found out, was a total misconception. But it led me to an interesting trivia item that is far from trivial to owners of large animals such as horses or cattle. Research revealed a sinister member of the usually beautiful Texas flora. This plant is even more sinister than one might expect, as its bloom is deceptively beautiful. A member of the genus Datura and the nightshade family, the herb grows in pastures, along roadsides, and in waste areas. The plants, which may grow as high as five feet, bear large, alternate, simple, irregularly blunt leaves, and very large, conspicuous, petunia-like flowers. The plant contains alkaloids that react with the nervous system to produce symptoms of incoherence, hallucinations, and incomprehension. John Reagor, D.V.M., at Texas A&M University told us that a horse eating the jimson weed will experience severe colic, and may die.

Interestingly, the weed's name comes not from the death of horses or other livestock, but directly from the poisoning of human beings. The name is a corruption of "Jamestown weed," and derives from the mass poisoning of soldiers sent to Jamestown, Virginia in 1676 to quell the uprising now known as Bacon's Rebellion. It is said that the soldiers inadvertently cooked and ate the greens and from then on the plant was called "Jamestown weed," gradually reduced to jimson weed. Steven Schwartzman's informative story "Speaking of Lesser known Texas wildflowers" in the April 2002 issue of *Texas Highways* was the source for much of our information about this sinister threat to Texas livestock. We are grateful to Mr. Schwartzman for permitting us to use his material for this trivia item.

THE LEGENDS AND LORE OF SOUTHWEST CONFERENCE FOOTBALL

One facet of Texas culture that has been the source of numerous legends, and more than its share of lore, is what was once almost a Texas cult, Southwest Conference football. Although the Southwest Conference no longer exists as it once was, it has left behind tracks that are just as visible and impressive as the dinosaur tracks that line the bottom of the Paluxy River in Glen Rose. These bits of football lore are sure to strike chords of nostalgia in the heart of Texas's myriad of old-time football fans, and serve to enlighten some of the newcomers to Texas college football. Those old-timers, who followed their favorite teams from the practice field to the New Year's Day game at Dallas's Cotton Bowl, may find a few surprises in this brief revelation of Texas football legends! College football, it seems, has been a vital part of Texas culture since its beginning. It has certainly spun off its share of unique bits of football lore that are worth capturing in print and preserving for future Texas football fanatics.

One such bit of lore is the poignant story of Texas A&M's 12th Man. All non-Aggies who attend an A&M football game for the first time are amazed to see the entire student body stand throughout the entire game, except at halftime, at which time they may sit. This college tradition has a most interesting and high-spirited background, which some find too strange to be true. Kern Tips's book *Football Texas Style* relates how this tradition is based on an event that took place in January of 1922 at the "Dixie Classics," which was the forerunner of today's Cotton Bowl game. The game was played at Dallas's Fair Park and pitted Texas A&M against Centre College, and it was a bitterly fought game. Tips reminds us that attrition due to injuries had depleted the A&M squad to the point that coach Dana Bible wasn't sure if he would have enough players to finish the game. Then the legendary A&M coach remembered seeing a player, E. King Gill, whom he had released from playing football to play his favorite sport, basketball, sitting in the stands. Coach Bible had Gill brought from the stands and suited up on the sidelines so he would be available to play if needed. Gill thus became the team's 12th man. With a show of school spirit, the entire student body becomes the school's 12th man and stands to show their willingness to play if needed!

Another great Texas football legend involves the naming of the University of Texas longhorn mascot, "BEVO." This usually ponderous longhorn steer owes his name to one of the university's fiercest rivals, Texas A&M. Research into the naming of the steer tells us that the U. of T. had lost a football game to the Aggies by the humiliating score of 13–0. And the Aggies were determined not to let the Longhorns forget the embarrassing defeat. To give the Longhorns an indelible reminder of the shameful loss, a group of Aggies traveled to Austin, home of the Longhorns, and stole the mascot, knowing that U.T. wouldn't have time to replace it before its next game. The Aggies branded the score 13–0 on the steer. The animal was then returned to the University of Texas at Austin. The embarrassed, but ingenious Longhorns had a "running iron" made (the type of iron used by rustlers to change existing brands). Using the iron they connected the 1 and 3 to form a B. They altered the dash to make an E and inserted a V before the 0. The result of these alterations was the word "BEVO." Since the word beeves means cattle, the Longhorns accepted the clandestinely obtained name for their mascot.

Another frequently asked football question is "How did the TCU Horned Frogs get their mascot?" This, too, is an interesting bit of lore. The *Handbook of Texas* explains it this way. Texas Christian University was originally Add-Ran Christian University.

In 1902 the name was changed to Texas Christian University. The school was located in Waco, Texas. In 1898, because the horned frog population on the campus was so great, the horned frog was selected as the name of the school's yearbook and football team. In 1910 the school's main building burned. Fort Worth offered the school a fifty-acre campus and $200,000 to move to their city. The university accepted the offer; so, after fifteen years in Waco the school moved to Fort Worth. With the noticeable absence of horned frogs, today, if the school were choosing a mascot, it would in all probability have to make another choice!

Believe it or not, the coveted Heisman trophy has Texas roots. This legendary football trophy was named for William Heisman, the first full-time football coach, and Athletic Director at Texas's Rice University from 1924 until 1927. The trophy is awarded annually to the most outstanding college football player in the United States.

THE LYNCHING OF SANTA CLAUS

There is nothing that can be remotely associated with the Christmas season that can, even vaguely, be related to the barbaric practice of lynching! Yet, a close study of our Texas trivia collection reveals a public record of an incident where the very symbol of the holiday was lynched by a West Texas mob. Folks who have read our book *A Treasury of Texas Trivia II* will perhaps recall what we wrote about the well-chronicled "Santa Claus Robbery" of the First National Bank in Cisco, Texas, in 1927. The bizarre incident has been grist for the typewriters of columnists and authors with an eye for the unusual for the past sixty-nine years. One aspect of the much publicized incident that has only been touched upon is the lynching of Marshall Ratliff (the Santa Claus bandit). For a review of that most unforgettable Christmas Eve, in 1927, we refer to one of the best books written about the event, *The Santa Claus Bank Robbery*, written by Ed Connel and first published by Longhorn Press in 1958. We gratefully acknowledge the publisher's permission to share a portion of their story with our readers.

In order to set the stage for the mob violence that led to the "necktie party" for Old Saint Nick, let us review the robbery itself.

Quoting from the aforementioned book: "The sun rose as bright as a day in May on that December 23, 1927 in the busy little town of Cisco, but, even with no prospects of a white Christmas, the citizens of this thriving town had caught the Yuletide spirit. Peace and goodwill rang in the hearts and faces of those who thronged the streets for their last minute Christmas purchases. The town's population seemed a melting pot of sun-tanned ranchers, oil field workers in their khakis, Mexican women in their black shawls, and fashionable ladies in the fashionable creations of the season. Cisco was aglow with Christmas—What with trees decorated and loaded with gifts in the windows, and other gaily colored decorations along the street. Of course, completing the picture, Santa Claus strolled leisurely down the sidewalk. He was surrounded by eager children flooding him with their wishes for Christmas. Noticing that Santa bore no signs or advertisements, one lady asked 'What store do you represent?' Quickly, Santa replied, 'You'll find out soon enough.' Santa sauntered unsuspectingly down the street, paused for a minute and entered the First National Bank. Following closely behind were Mrs. B. P. Blassengame, and her six-year-old daughter, Frances. Little Frances, seeing Santa across the street, had insisted that her mother take her over to talk with him. The usual activities were in progress in the bank. When Alex Spears, bank cashier, smiled and greeted the red-suited man, in the bank, the cry 'Stick-Em Up!' rang out. Around the room were three men with drawn pistols. They had entered the bank while Santa Claus was the center of attention. Santa forced bank officials to open the safe, as customers and employees were lined up against the wall."

The book gives all the bloody details about the ensuing shootout with police, who had quickly, after being alerted, surrounded the bank. The carnage that followed resulted in the deaths or injury of eleven persons, both citizens and bandits, that unforgettable Christmas in 1927. Here we refer again to *The Santa Claus Bank Robbery*. "One of those seriously wounded in the Wild West type shoot-out was the costumed Santa Claus. A posse caught up with the surviving bandits the following day. Trials for the Santa Claus bandits netted them harsh sentences. The red-suited leader, Marshall Ratliff, was sentenced to die in Huntsville's electric chair. In a subsequent attempt to escape from jail while in Cisco for a sanity hearing, Ratliff killed still another Cisco officer, 'Uncle Tom' Jones, one of the jailers. This old-time officer was loved by the townspeople of Cisco. His death proved to be Santa Claus' undoing! Citizens hearing of the shooting of the popular lawman, soon began to gather at the jail with blood in their eyes. The violence poured out upon this law-abiding Texas town, by these sociopaths, was enough to rekindle the 'code of the Old West' in the minds and hearts of the otherwise peace-loving folks, who had just seen a number of their citizens killed by the bandits led by this now convicted mad-dog in a Santa suit! The murmur of 'We want action!' turned into a cry and then into action. The surviving jailer was overpowered and taken by several men. His keys were seized and the men flew up the stairs of the second floor. Some 15 or 20 men entered the jail. They wanted Ratliff. They took the Santa Claus bandit to a vacant lot almost a block away. A throng of spectators followed the little group that carried Ratliff. They came to a halt just steps from a theater in town where, ironically, was playing, a stage play entitled 'Noose.' This time, however, it was no play, it was real. A rope was looped around Ratliff's neck and thrown over a guy wire running between two telephone poles. Several hands caught the rope and lifted Ratliff (Santa Claus) into the air. He dangled for a moment, before the rope broke and he fell to the ground murmuring, 'God have mercy and forgive me.' The lynchers of Eastland County found a new rope stronger than the first. As he was being pulled up for the second time, he was asked if he wanted to talk? 'Let me down and I'll talk,' he answered. The rope was slackened. The only words the crowd could understand was, 'Forgive me boys.' The last time he was lifted some fifteen feet into the air and the rope did not break. His form dangled in the moonlight until Judge Clyde Garrett ordered the body taken down. Before his death, 'Uncle Tom' Jones was told that Ratliff had been put to death."

WATERSKIING IN A TEXAS OIL TANK

"Big" and "Oil" are as synonymous with Texas as "cold" and "gold" are with Alaska. And, unbelievable as it sounds, and it probably

This bird's-eye view of the million-barrel oil tank in Monahans, Texas shows the immense size of this Texas oil tank. The two-story Holman House in the background gives some perspective of the tank's size. This photo is provided by the Ward County Historical Society Commission. We are grateful to this commission for providing this photo and some facts about the tank.

would be in any state other than Texas, these two adjectives have teamed up to give us one of our most graphic illustrations of Texas bigness, and without one ounce of Texas exaggeration! There was a time in recent Texas history that West Texas had an oil storage tank large enough that one could enjoy the sport of waterskiing on it. To fully appreciate this story, turn back the pages of time to the West Texas oil boom of 1928. Oil was being produced out of the West Texas soil faster than it could be shipped out. The Shell Oil Company constructed a huge in-ground oil storage tank in Monahans, Texas. The million-barrel oil tank measures 522 feet across and its walls were 35 feet high. Creosote-soaked posts supported a wire-mesh-reinforced concrete dome. The builders left a six-foot space between the top of the wall and the dome to be cooled by West Texas breezes. The tank was built to hold 1,084,000 barrels of crude oil. Construction of the giant oil tank was completed in ninety days at the cost of a quarter of a million dollars. Calculations, said a fact sheet, were made with an abacus in the hands of a Chinese engineer from California where Shell had built another tank. The tank was filled only once, as it was detected that the oil level was falling. It was first believed that the giant tank was leaking, but an inspection proved otherwise. It was determined that the oil was evaporating. Use of the giant holding tank was discontinued when the Great Depression caused the price of oil to drop to five cents a barrel. Shell set up pumps and sold off the crude to avoid any further drop in value.

In 1958 Wayne Long and his wife, Amelie, bought the giant oil tank and surrounding land, envisioning turning the giant tank into a recreational lake where swimming and boating could be enjoyed in the arid West Texas region. Wayne Long drilled six water wells and pumped water into the tank from the aquifer that runs under the Monahans region. Opening day of the West Texas oil tank "lake" was very successful, featuring waterskiing, boating, and a water show. Like the oil tank, the recreational addition to West Texas was a short-lived success, as the water level in the tank suddenly dropped. Again a leak was suspected, but an inspection revealed the water loss was due to evaporation. After all, the new lake was situated in the northern part of the Chihuahuan desert. The recreation project was abandoned in 1984.

Mrs. Long gave the tank to the county. It became a sesquicentennial project. The tank became the Million Barrel Museum, which opened in 1987. The big hole lined with concrete now safeguards relics and mementos of days gone by. The million-barrel oil tank now plays host to community and private barbecues, dances, and chili cook-offs. A visit to the Million Barrel Museum not only allows the visitor to see the Texas-size oil tank that was big enough for swimming and boating, but also to step back in time. One can return to the 1920s West Texas lifestyle and see housing and farming equipment. It is truly Texas bigness to have an oil tank large enough to have a boat ramp, as this tank once did! The Museum is located at 400 Museum Blvd., Monahans, Texas. Telephone (915) 943-8401.

Dallas's purported John Neely Bryan cabin. Photo by Marianne Cannon.

THE JOHN NEELY BRYAN CABIN: A DALLAS LEGEND THAT MAY BE A MYTH

If you've driven in the heart of the metropolis of Dallas, Texas, and rubbed your eyes in disbelief upon seeing an ancient log cabin in the pioneer style sitting smack dab in the middle of the county government section of the city, feel comforted in knowing that your eyes weren't playing tricks on you, nor had the Texas sun addled your otherwise lucid brain! What you were seeing is one of Dallas's historical legends, the reputed home of the city's founder, John Neely Bryan. This relic from the days of the city's founding in 1841 is as much an icon to Dallas's residents as the Flying Red Horse that has been perched atop what was the Magnolia Building since the 1934 convention of the National Petroleum Association. No! You were not witnessing a mirage when you first saw the old relic, as you might have thought. But, if you are one of the many die-hard loyalists who hold on to the belief that Dallas's founder actually, at one time, resided in the primitive structure, you may be believing a myth! Although we, like many others, hold a certain reverence and respect for this faux city symbol, because it was, most definitely, resided in by one of the county's earliest residents and deserves its place in the category of Dallas County icons, we are forced to join the throng of researchers who are unable to find evidentiary records to place Mr. Bryan in this old cabin. It is not our wish to flippantly deflate the balloons of those civic-minded believers in the idea that old John maintained his personal household in the cabin that now rests in the shadows of "Old Red," the county's nineteenth-century courthouse on the corner of Elm and Market Streets. But, in our search for historical truth, we would like to offer the following facts that lead us to our unpopular conclusion.

Our sleuthing into the origin of the primitive old Dallas icon started out on a trail that had grown as cold as last week's clabber! But the first clues provided much insight into the origin of the "John Neely Bryan" cabin. We discovered that the cabin had been given to Dallas County for the Texas Centennial in 1936 by Buckner's Orphan's Home. This Dallas institution suggested we read Dr. Karen Bullock's biography of "Father" R. C. Buckner, *Homeward Bound*. This lovingly written book provided the first gold nuggets in our dig to find the history of Dallas's "John Neely Bryan" log cabin. After "Father" Buckner first opened the orphans' home on a modest scale, the need soon overtook the capacity of the original facility. Dr. Bullock writes that a search for land on which to expand led R. C. Buckner to a piece of "black prairie land eight miles east of Dallas." J. T. Pinson, owner of the land, sold the property to "Father" Buckner. The deed was filed in Dallas September 25, 1880. It is here that we find the first reference to what probably was the log cabin now accepted by most, and venerated by some, as John Neely Bryan's home. Dr. Bullock writes as follows: "Board members E. F. Brown, J. R. Rogers, J. M. Graves, Sam Smith, and L. H. Tillman, joined Buckner at the site to survey and dedicate the land. There on the 27th of September, in the small cedar log cabin, inhabited by a share-cropper's family, the men and women knelt to dedicate the property to the Lord in prayer." The log cabin referred to in this poignant scene obviously existed on the Pinson property at the time he sold it to "Father" Buckner. If Mr. Pinson was under the impression that the old log cabin was once the home of the founder of Dallas, there is no written record to that effect. There was, obviously, some who must have believed, whatever the reason, that the cabin purchased with the Pinson land was, indeed, the home of John Neely Bryan, for Dr. Bullock provides the first clue linking the old cabin to Dallas's founder. She writes as follows: "The Dallas County Historical Society formally petitioned the Home for the John Neely Bryan cabin, which had stood on the Buckner property in 1879 when it was purchased by 'Father' Buckner. The Society was planning Dallas' Texas Centennial for the following year and wished to restore and preserve the cabin for the county. The Board voted unanimously to give the historical cabin to Dallas County on 23rd April." It seems obvious that the Dallas Historical Society felt strongly enough that the cabin was once the home of Bryan, that it made efforts to bring it under its supervision.

All that we actually learned about the so-called Bryan cabin from Buckner's biography was that the cabin now on display in the 600 block of Dallas's Elm Street is the cabin that was once on the property owned by Buckner's Orphan's Home, and which the Home presented to Dallas County in 1936. We should take note of the fact that the land on which the cabin was located was, according to the Buckner biography, "eight miles east of Dallas." This, in the 1840s, was a substantial distance for Bryan to travel if this cabin was his home. Certainly the city's developer would have need to stay in close contact with his developing town. Adding to the inability to verify the authenticity of the Bryan cabin is an item found in the April 15th, 1996 edition of the *Dallas Morning News* announcing the county's plans for celebrating its 150th anniversary. In referring to Bryan's cabin, the article says, "Historians say the cabin never belonged to the city founder, John Neely Bryan, as county folklorists like to claim."

Another nail driven into the coffin of the Bryan legend is provided by the remembrances of someone who ought to know, a contemporary of Bryan and one of Dallas's first settlers, if not *the* first, James J. Beeman. Mr. Beeman was the great-great-grandfather of my friend, Marti Wise of Garland. Ms. Wise was kind enough to give me access to James Beeman's memoirs. James Beeman came to Texas in 1840. He and his brother, John Beeman, were settled in at Bird's Fort when "Col. John Neely Bryan persuaded them to visit his newly founded city on the Trinity, in hopes of selling them on the idea of settling there," and convince them he did! James Beeman's testimony about Bryan's home in the fledgling new town should be viewed as credible, because on February 23rd, 1843 Bryan married Beeman's niece, Margaret. Perhaps it is what James Beeman didn't say that points a historic finger of suspicion at the legend that Bryan's home was the cabin next to Dallas's old courthouse! It was customary in those times for a suitor to have a home prepared for his intended before they married. Although he went to great lengths to describe, in detail, the various homes and blockhouses built at the time of Dallas's birth, James Beeman makes absolutely no reference to the residence of John Neely Bryan, which he and Margaret were to call home! The *Handbook of Texas*, considered by most Texas historians as the final authority on Texas history, has one reference to Bryan building a log cabin in his new town of Dallas. This reference pertains to the town's early settlers, Captain Mable Gilbert and his wife. The Gilberts were contemporaries of John and Jim Beeman and accompanied them with Col. Bryan to look over his new town. The *Handbook* says: "The Gilbert family became one of the earliest to settle the community that was to become Dallas, and Mrs. Gilbert was the first Anglo-American woman to live there. Bryan constructed a log cabin for them at a site that became the foot of Main Street in Dallas." Wherever the original Main Street was! This is the only reference we have found relating to Bryan constructing a cabin in Dallas, although we concede that writings indicate that he "settled" near the Trinity, which would necessitate a place in which to live. Some might contend the cabin on display next to the old red courthouse might be the cabin built by Bryan for the Gilberts, were it not for the fact that we know this cabin was given to Dallas County by Buckner's Orphan's Home, and was on that property when "Father" Buckner bought the land, which was certainly not at the "foot of Main Street"!

One thing that bolsters our contention that John Neely Bryan never lived in the "Bryan cabin" in Dallas is a letter we discovered in Margaret Thetford's *Dallas Morning News* column, "Family Tree," of December 10, 1983. Mrs. J. M. Hacksma of Wanatchee,

Washington wrote that her ancestor, Gideon Pemberton, "owned the land where the Buckner Orphans Home was later built and had his home and wagon shop on the property." Mrs. Hacksma, says the column, "claims the log cabin that stands today near the Old Red courthouse, was the Pemberton home and was moved from the Pemberton land to the downtown location." The column indicates that, according to Mrs. Hacksma, "The property was sold to the Rev. Pinson, and Pinson re-sold the property to Rev. Buckner." We were able to track down eighty-three-year-old Mrs. Jim Hacksma on August 17, 2001 in the beautiful Washington apple country of Wanatchee. We talked about her letter to the *Dallas Morning News*. Mrs. Hacksma stated she had seen the records where the Buckner's Orphan's Home land was deeded by Sam Houston to the Pemberton family, which were her ancestors. She was adamant that "the cabin purported to be the 'Bryan cabin' was built and lived in by the Pembertons and was the first house built in Dallas." She said, "At no time did John Neely Bryan live in the cabin."

It is our contention that in the days of 1841, when this entrepreneur was making every effort to promote his new town, he would not have built, and lived in, a cabin that would have distanced him from his town by eight miles! We located only one semiofficial pronouncement that the cabin we Dallasites have associated with our city's founder actually belonged to John Neely Bryan. The Dallas Chapter of the American Institute of Architects published a brochure entitled "A Guide to Dallas Architecture," which included the downtown Dallas Historic District. The caption under a photo of the "John Neely Bryan cabin" reads as follows: "John Neely Bryan cabin c. 1845 600 block of Elm Street. Records suggest that this is the last of three cabins, and the first permanent home erected by Dallas' entrepreneurial founder. Constructed from many of the original hewn cedar logs, the cabin was actually one half of the original 'dog-trot' structure (two enclosed rooms separated by a covered open porch). This remnant of Bryan's pioneer settlement served for years as the center of the social, political, and economic life in Dallas." We contacted several members of this respected professional group, but none could direct us to sources where these claims could be verified. There is little question about this cabin being one of the first buildings in

John Neely Bryan's town called Dallas. But there is, in our opinion, reason to question its being built and lived in by the city's founder. This popular Dallas legend may well be a myth! In a recent conversation with former Dallas mayor pro tem Don Hicks, Hicks agreed that it was doubtful that John Neely Bryan ever lived in the old cabin on Elm Street.

DISPUTE OVER GOOSE'S NEST LEADS TO DESTRUCTION OF GRAYSON COUNTY COURTHOUSE

While reading *A History of Grayson County* by Mattie D. Lucas and Mita H. Hall, we learned how a dispute over the location of a goose's nest resulted in the demolition of the Grayson County courthouse. The bizarre episode in Grayson County history was explained by the authors as follows: "In the latter part of 1858, a champagne supper was held in Sherman honoring John Butterfield and his associates of the Overland Mail. The celebrants began to argue about the location of the nest of an old gray goose. A number contended that the nest was under the old log courthouse and to prove their point, they led the crowd to the courthouse and proceeded to tear it down and proudly displayed the nest! Bets were freely made while the demolition was going on, and music furnished by a banjo player whose fingers were made exceptionally nimble by the champagne." Although not included in the authors' account of the destruction of the courthouse, it is implied and confirmed by local historians that the participants in the destruction of the courthouse were somewhat driven by the champagne. We are grateful to the family of Mita Hall for granting us permission to reprint this story from her fine book.

BIG! EVEN BY TEXAS STANDARDS (TEXAS LOSES PECAN TREE CROWN)

Texas's claim to having the nation's largest pecan tree (our official state tree) had to be surrendered to the state of Tennessee.

The defending champion, located on the property of Billy Finch in Weatherford, Texas, was 91 feet tall and 254 inches around, which is REALLY BIG, even by Texas standards. The size can better be imagined if one knows it would take eleven people standing shoulder to shoulder to surround the trunk. Although the tree's age is a mystery (no one being foolish enough to want to cut it down to count the rings), experts have estimated the tree to be 400 to 500 years old. The Texas tree has a bigger spread, 120 feet, to Tennessee's 111 feet. But that isn't enough to retain the title. Texas's only hope is a fatalistic one. Steve Houser, a local arborist, was quoted in the *Dallas Morning News* as saying, "The sad thing is that when trees are big enough to be champions, they are nearing the end of their healthy lives. They can be brittle and susceptible to disease and bad weather. If lightning strikes in Tennessee, we could be taking out the tape measure again."

FANNIN COUNTY'S FOUR-WHEELED STORM CELLAR

Over the years we have discovered that the search for noteworthy trivia about the Lone Star State is very much akin to an archaeological dig! One may start out excavating a particular site, or subject, and as the layers of information surrounding the subject are painstakingly scraped away and meticulously sifted, they often yield artifacts of great value to the trivia collector. Most of these nuggets of trivia are not visible to the naked eye and would go undiscovered were it not for the pursuit of the mother lode. Such was the case in our recent in-depth study of one of Texas's most laughable communities, the Fannin County town of Bug Tussle. I say "laughable" because the very mention of its name evokes chuckles and usually eyebrows raised in disbelief! But yes, there is really a town named Bug Tussle. And its story can be found within the pages of this book of legends and lore. It was during my numerous interviews with former "Bug Tusslers" that I learned the heart-warming story of a true, personal religious experience at the Bug Tussle cotton gin.

But this poignant trivia gem sifted from the layers of East Texas soil that surrounds the tiny town with the comical name was not the only artifact uncovered during our Bug Tussle "dig." Somewhat on the lighter side was my discovery of Fannin County's "four-wheeled storm cellar." A publication produced by East Texas State University at Commerce included an article on Bug Tussle by Mark Jones. In Mr. Jones's excellent coverage of Bug Tussle, he piqued our interest by telling the story of that community's "four-wheeled storm cellar." Mr. Jones told how a family named Green occupied Judge Fink's store after it had been abandoned. Mr. Green was a tinkerer, who worked on small engines and other mechanical and electrical things. Mr. Green had previously bought old automobiles and salvaged parts from them. He even buried an old car, believed to be a late 1940s model, beside the store, to be used as a storm shelter. According to Jones, the car was still there, its roof protruding out of the ground a few feet beside the store. Mr. Jones's article was written in the late 1970s, and time has taken its toll. Recent exploration at the store reveals that the "four-wheeled storm cellar" is no longer visible. Storm cellars are commonplace in rural Texas, including Fannin County, but it is highly unlikely that the use of an automobile as a storm cellar exists elsewhere in the vast state of Texas. "Only in Bug Tussle!" one might be prone to say. We are glad indeed that Mr. Jones saw fit to preserve this morsel of trivia, which we feel deserves inclusion in this book of Texas legend and lore. We are grateful to the Journalism Department of East Texas State University for granting us permission to use these excerpts from its publication.

In a recent conversation with Henry "Junior" James of Bonham, James told the author that his uncle, Henry Green, was responsible for creating this unique storm cellar. He said that in the late 1950s, tinkerer Green buried the Dodge panel van, which he believed was a late 1940s model. When asked why his uncle decided that this old car would make a good storm cellar, "Junior" said his uncle bought old cars and salvaged parts from them. He had previously buried a car for a storm cellar at his home in Honey Grove, Texas. Mr. James said he didn't know if the Bug Tussle storm cellar had ever been used.

The Alamo Street Restaurant and Dinner Theater, designed in mission style architecture, was completed in 1912. It is in the historic King William District of San Antonio. The appearance of the specters during theater performances may be disconcerting to some, but there are those who attend this popular restaurant in hopes of being treated to a visit from the world beyond. Marcia Larsen was kind enough to furnish this photo of her unique addition to the Alamo City's already exciting nightlife.

SAN ANTONIO GHOST A STICKLER FOR THEATER DECORUM

Not only is the Alamo Street Restaurant and Theater in San Antonio well known in this "Mother-lode" of Texas history, for its downright good "stick-to-your-ribs" home cooking, and its theatrical performances presented in the church's sanctuary, guests are sometimes treated to an appearance of one of the four ghosts that haunt the mission-style building built in 1912 as the Alamo Methodist Church (if an apparition of folks long dead can be considered a treat). Marcia Larsen, who, with her brother, William, bought the old building in 1976, told us that several psychics have identified several of the ethereal visitors and provided background information on them. One ghost who makes regular appearances was an actress named Margaret Gathing who died in 1975. The ghost started appearing in 1976. She generally appears during a theatrical presentation in the Alamo City's unique dinner theater, sometimes shushing patrons who talk during the performance. She is seen by numerous patrons when she decides to show up. The deceased actress lived a block from the old building. Ms. Larsen told us that "docents working in the ghost's earthly residence, which is now a museum, report that the late actress has not been seen at her home since her death." Another of the apparitions at the Alamo Street Restaurant and Theater is that of a boy who died of polio in the 1950s, said Ms. Larsen. The boy's only connection to the building was that he was cared for by church members at a time when care was much needed. Contrary to the ghost of Margaret Gathing, the young polio victim's ghost has not been seen! Only his boylike mischievous antics, which include, but are not limited to, throwing dishes, betray his presence! The Alamo Street Restaurant and Theater is located at 1150 S. Alamo Street in San Antonio. A word of caution: Better not talk during performances unless your nerves will withstand a gentle reprimand from the beyond.

HIZZONER THE GOAT

One bit of Texas lore that sounds truly too bizarre to be true is the true story of the West Texas town that elected a beer-drinking goat mayor. Some may be tempted to say, "Sounds just like our mayor!", but in the Brewster County town of Lajitas, it is politically correct to call the mayor an old goat! For a goat he is! The otherwise nondescript town of Lajitas, which sits snug against Mexico's northern border, is described in the *Handbook of Texas* as "overlooking the Rio Grande at the San Carlos Ford of the Comanche Trail." Its inhabitants, says the *Handbook*, were Mexican Indians for years. They were driven from the area by the Comanche during the eighteenth and nineteenth centuries. Anglo-Americans first arrived in the mid-1800s. Located at the western edge of the Big Bend National Park, the border town became a point of interest to

Clay Henry III (Hizzoner the Goat) was elected mayor of Lajitas, Texas in 1999. Thanks to photographer Sam Richardson of Terlingua, Texas and to Anne Bingham of the Lajitas Resort and Club for her assistance in gathering facts about Texas's most unusual mayor. Clay Henry is further proof that often in Texas, truth is stranger than fiction!

tourists. The town that blended in with the rugged Coahuilan desert is not bereft of history. The *Handbook* reminds us that "in 1916 the interruption of commerce by the bandits of Francisco (Pancho) Villa brought General John J. 'Blackjack' Pershing's troops to Lajitas, where they established a major cavalry post."

In the 1980s a motel stood on the actual foundations of the post. The Lajitas property has changed hands several times. In 1990, the town's population was reported as fifty. In 1985 the Big Bend region, including Lajitas, became an increasingly popular site for shooting movies. The unincorporated town of Lajitas and 25,000 surrounding acres were bought by Austin multimillionaire Steve Smith. Included in the deal was the popular Lajitas Trading Post. Living in a pen next to the Trading Post was Clay Henry III, a goat. Developer Smith acquired Clay Henry III along with the Trading Post. The goat brought some ambience to the little West Texas town when it was discovered he had a penchant for drinking beer. Anne Bingham, Director of Communications for Lajitas Resort and Club, advised us that Clay Henry prefers a cold Texas-brewed Lone Star Beer, but would imbibe most brands of suds, including cerveza imported from nearby Mexico!

In 1999, the four-year-old beer-drinking tourist attraction was nominated to run against Clyde, the town's stable dog, in Lajitas's mayoral election. A poll tax of $1 was instituted for this election as a fund-raiser, said Ms. Bingham. Over $2,000 was raised for a local charity. Clay Henry outdrew Clyde in votes and became Lajitas's mayor. When asked if Hizzoner the Goat had any civic responsibilities other than entertaining the town's influx of tourists, Ms. Bingham replied that he had no other official duties. If developer Steve Smith's resort plans for Lajitas mature as expected, Clay Henry III will become one of Texas's most popular mayors. He may be faced with the distinct possibility of alcoholism! To our knowledge Lajitas, Texas is the only U.S. town having a billy goat for a mayor. Clay Henry is the proud father of two kids, which may portend a political dynasty for the Brewster County town of Lajitas! It is fairly obvious that this West Texas town does not take its local politics seriously. Look out, Austin! Lajitas has proved that, indeed, truth is stranger than fiction!

ABOUT THE AUTHOR

For over ten years, native Texan Bill Cannon, a retired detective, has been a radio personality on radio station KAAM. It was his Texas trivia questions broadcast by this station that resulted in his two previous Texas trivia books, *A Treasury of Texas Trivia* and *A Treasury of Texas Trivia II*. Dallas area residents followed his weekly newspaper column, “Wudja Believe,” in the *Metro News*. Sought after as a luncheon and after-dinner speaker, Bill Cannon seasoned his speeches with Texas humor stories, which were compiled in his 1999 book, *A Treasury of Texas Humor*. His *Tales from Toadsuck, Texas* allows us Texans to laugh at ourselves through the antics of the unsophisticated small-town residents of Toadsuck! The typically Texas names of his characters in this real Texas town produce as many chuckles as the town's name produces. Bill continues to use his detective instincts to ferret out the unusual, little-known, and forgotten facts that add to the mystique of the Lone Star State.